Scotland's leading educational publishers

Standard Grade
History

✗ Colin Bagnall ✗

Contents

Unit IIC: International co-operation and conflict, 1930s–1960s

Unit IIIC: Russia, 1914–1941

Unit IIID: Germany, 1918–1939

How to use this revision guide

Hitting the target

Now that you have made the wise decision of buying this guide you will probably have several key aims in mind. The first and most important of these will be the best grade that you can achieve in your Standard Grade. You may also wish to improve your skills and gain knowledge that will help you in life and work later on. You may simply enjoy finding out as much as you can about how things got to be the way they are. Studying History can do all of these things for you. Since this is a revision guide it will focus on the first of these most of all, but it is important that you are clear about what you want to get out of your revision if you are to get the most out of this book. If you can get satisfaction and even enjoyment from the process of preparing yourself for Standard Grade History, then your task will be so much easier.

This guide is not the same as your textbook. It assumes that you have studied the topics before. This book will provide you with three things that will help you maximise your chances of meeting your Standard Grade History targets.

The first of these is the key information about events and ideas that you will have to write about in the examination. In the sections of the examination entitled 'Knowledge and Understanding' you will have to recall and organise these key pieces of information to score marks. In the sections called 'Enquiry skills' this information will help you understand the source extracts and provide you with additional points that you can make in response to questions about the sources.

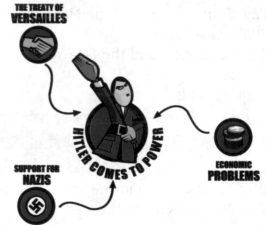

The second part of the exam that the book will help you with is to do with the kinds of skills that help you get as many marks as possible in the examination. There will be tips and guidance about how to answer questions as well as you can, and sample questions that allow you to practise. This guide is aimed at General and Credit level, and it will tell you which information is specifically for Credit candidates.

A mind map will help you visualise and organise your understanding of a particular topic, so that you can see clearly how one idea or event relates to other ideas and events.

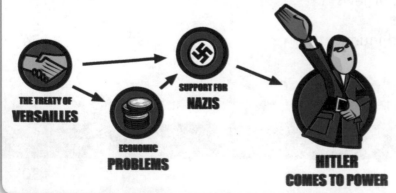

A flow chart shows a sequence of events. This flow chart shows Hitler's rise to power in Germany.

Finally the book will help you through the revision process by giving you ideas, exercises and revision games that will keep you thinking actively while you revise. Three of the useful exercises you can use are 'mind maps', 'flow diagrams' and 'ripple diagrams'. The illustrations on page 4 and below explain how these work.

At the start of each section, set yourself a target for how well you would like to understand the topic on a scale of one to ten. As you complete each section, give your understanding of the topic a rating out of ten. If your rating is less than seven, you might need to give that topic another look. If your rating is seven or more you can congratulate yourself on hitting your target.

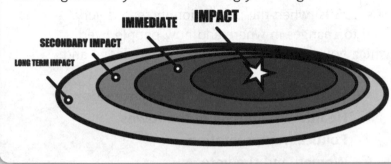

IMPACT

IMMEDIATE

SECONDARY IMPACT

LONG TERM IMPACT

With a ripple diagram you imagine that an event or an individual is a pebble thrown into a still pond. You can picture how important they were in influencing later events by writing immediate, secondary and long term impacts in concentric circles spreading outwards.

Assessment summary

You will be assessed through an examination in May. This will consist of two papers. You will be entered either for the Foundation and General Paper or for the General and Credit Paper. In doing the Foundation Paper you can achieve only a grade 5 or 6, for the General Paper only a grade 3 or 4 and for the Credit Paper only a grade 1 or 2. Make sure that you know which papers you are entered for and when you need to be at the examination venue.

Each paper will have ten topic areas across the three units. Make sure that you can find the topics that you are doing quickly. Because there are so many options in the exam booklet it is a very good idea at the start of the exam to underline or highlight the topics that you will tackle and their page numbers in the booklet.

Each topic is divided into a knowledge and understanding section and an enquiry skills question. The marks are weighted heavily towards the enquiry skills questions, so make sure that you get plenty of practice with these kinds of questions. Each section of this book gives you a chance to rehearse these skills.

Top Tip
Get hold of a copy of Leckie & Leckie's collection of past papers to familiarise yourself with the exam in advance and practise the type of questions that you will do in the exam.

Course units

There are three units in the Standard Grade course. You must choose to do one topic from each unit.

Unit 1

Unit I of the examination will test how well you understand in what ways and for what reasons Britain changed over a period of around 100 years. You should make sure that your answers in this section discuss changes and the reasons for them.

Unit IB examines a period in Britain (1830s–1930s) when the population increased very quickly and when changes in technology led to changes in where and how people lived and worked. There are several areas in which you will need to show your knowledge and understanding:

- **Population and migration**
- **The Highland Clearances**
- **Coal mining**
- **Railways**
- **Employment and working conditions**
- **Health and housing in the countryside**
- **Health and housing in the towns**
- **Political representation**
- **Women and the vote**

Unit IC is similar to Unit IB, except that it covers the period 1880 to the present day. During this time the population grew in different ways, and new industries such as shipbuilding and the motor car became important. There is some overlap with Unit 1B. There are several areas in which you will need to show your knowledge and understanding:

- **Population and migration**
- **Shipbuilding**
- **The motor car**
- **Women at work**
- **Trade unions**
- **Health and housing**
- **Political representation and votes for women**

Unit 2

Unit 2 of the examination will test how well you understand the causes of conflict and co-operation between nations, with the topics covered in this book focusing on the twentieth century.

Topic IIB focuses mainly on events surrounding the First World War. You will need to have a clear idea about the events that led the world to war in 1914, the key aspects of life on the Western and Home Fronts and how nations attempted to restore stability and peace to the world afterwards.

There are several areas in which you will need to show your knowledge and understanding:

- **Long term causes of war**
- **Short term causes of war**
- **The battlefield on the Western Front**
- **A soldier's life on the Western Front**
- **The Home Front in Britain**
- **The Home Front in Germany and the end of the war**
- **The Treaty of Versailles**
- **The League of Nations and peacekeeping in the 1920s**

Topic IIC concentrates mainly on events surrounding the Second World War. You will need to have a clear idea about the events that led the world to war, some key aspects of the war itself, and the attempts after the war to avoid the emerging Cold War conflict. There are several areas in which you will need to show your knowledge and understanding:

- **Hitler's foreign policy**
- **Appeasement**
- **The Home Front in Britain**
- **The Home Front in Germany**
- **Weapons and tactics**
- **The decline of Britain**
- **The rise of the superpowers**
- **The United Nations**
- **Problems in Berlin**
- **The Cuban missile crisis**

Unit 3

Unit 3 of the course requires you to examine the history of one country in depth. The two countries covered in this book are Russia and Germany.

Topic IIIC looks at Russia during the turbulent years when it was transformed through violent revolution from a country ruled by an autocrat called the Tsar, into a Communist dictatorship under the rule of Joseph Stalin. You will need to show a good knowledge and understanding of several areas:

- **The Tsar's Russia 1: nation and government**
- **The Tsar's Russia 2: Russian society**
- **The First World War and the fall of the Tsar**
- **The Provisional Government**
- **The Bolsheviks take over**
- **Civil war**
- **War Communism and the New Economic Policy**
- **Stalin takes over**
- **Collectivisation and the Five Year Plans**
- **Purges**

Topic IIID looks at Germany in the traumatic years between the wars when a defeated and embittered country attempted to recover from the disaster of the First World War only to meet with the disaster of the Great Depression that pushed Germany into the hands of Hitler's Nazi dictatorship. You will need to show a good knowledge and understanding of several areas:

- **War, humiliation and the impact of the Treaty of Versailles**
- **The Weimar Republic: a new start?**
- **Revolts**
- **Hyperinflation**
- **Depression**
- **The rise of the Nazis**
- **Nazi Government**
- **The Nazis in power 1: the treatment of Jews**
- **The Nazis in power 2: young people**
- **The Nazis in power 3: militarism and intimidation**
- **Opposition**

Population and migration

Definitions

Population means the number of people living in the country.

Migration means how people moved around as time went on.

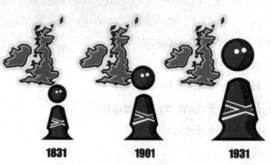

The population of Scotland was 2.3 million in 1831, 4.5 million by 1901 and 4.8 million by 1931.

The population of Great Britain as a whole was 16.2 million in 1831, 37 million by 1901 and 45 million by 1931.

The main reasons for population change

The main reasons for the increase in population between 1831 and 1931 are shown below:

A rise in the number of people being born (birth rate)

- People began marrying younger and so had larger families.
- Food became more plentiful and varied so people were healthier and stronger.
- Improvements in the conditions of towns (**housing** and **hygiene**) and better medicines meant that more children survived and grew up to have families of their own.

People were living longer (higher life expectancy)

- As the life expectancy increased, people started to have smaller families in the towns as laws prevented children working, and having fewer children allowed a better standard of living for families. This meant that the increase in population slowed down.

Increasing immigration

- There was increasing immigration from the middle of the 1800s, especially from Ireland.

The rising population was partly caused by and led to migration. There was **emigration** from Scotland because of events such as the **Highland Clearances**. There was **immigration**, particularly from Ireland following the **Great Famine**.

Irish immigration

From the 1840s hundreds of thousands of Irish people fled famine, hunger and unemployment. Tens of thousands of them came to Britain, and especially to Scotland, leading to the rapid growth of cities such as Glasgow and Dundee.

- The failure of the potato crop in Ireland from 1845–50 had a devastating effect on the population as they depended on potatoes to live. Hundreds of thousands of people died, and in the years after, many of those who could left the country.

- At its peak in the mid-1800s the Irish-born population of Scotland was around 7 per cent, about twice the percentage of the Irish population of England.

- The majority settled in the West of Scotland, in Ayrshire, Dumbarton, Renfrew and Lanark, but some also settled in the East in Dundee, Edinburgh and Leith.

- The Irish often took unskilled jobs, such as labouring, harvesting and factory work, undercutting the wages of the native Scottish population. This caused some resentment.

- The majority of Irish immigrants were Catholic, leading to conflict with the local Protestant population, which increased further when Protestant Irish immigrants also arrived in Glasgow.

Top Tip

When revising it is often useful to look at something new to freshen things up. This book gives you the essentials, but in addition, two websites that you might find useful are: bbc.co.uk/scotland/education (click on History, then 'Immigrants and Exiles') or spartacus.schoolnet.co.uk and look for Irish immigration.

Quick Test

1. By how much did the population of Britain grow between 1831 and 1931?

2. Why did people getting married earlier lead to a higher population?

3. Give three other reasons why the population grew.

4. Write two banner headlines as if you were the editor of a Scottish newspaper in 1901 and in 1931, reporting the figures from the population Census for those two years. Highlight what the most remarkable thing about each of these figures is.

Did you hit your target for this topic? Give yourself a mark out of ten.

Answers 1. Around 29 million (28.8 million to be precise) **2.** They could have more children **3.** Diet, housing and hygiene improved; people began to live longer; immigration

The Highland Clearances

Highland migration

Throughout the 1800s thousands of Scottish Highlanders left their **crofts** (small farms) and went to live in towns, in cities or abroad to Canada, the USA, New Zealand and other countries.

- In the early 1800s, half of the population of Scotland lived in the Highlands.
- By the 1930s over two thirds of the population lived in towns and cities.
- The Highlanders left for a combination of PULL factors and PUSH factors.
- The crofts were replaced with sheep farms and leisure activities such as hunting.

Top Tip

Migration always takes place because of a combination of PUSH factors (reasons that drive people to move) and PULL factors (reasons that attract people to new areas).

CREDIT

Pull	Push
Jobs	Bad weather and infertile land
A better climate	Landowners evicted crofters
Cheap and fertile land	Charities organised emigration
Travel was becoming easier	
Relatives had gone before	

The role of landowners

People disagree about whether the Clearances were carried out by harsh and unjust landowners, as there are some arguments in favour of the landowners' actions. You might be asked to identify or compare these views when they appear in sources in the exam.

Some people say landowners were unjust because:

- they only cared about making money, and sheep made bigger profits than crofters paying rent.
- the factors (men who worked for the landowners) were brutal in throwing crofters off their land; they often burned the cottages down.
- the journey, especially overseas, was difficult; many people suffered and many died.

Others say that the landowners' actions can be defended because:

- the Highlands were overpopulated and the land was not good enough to support the number of people who lived there.
- many crofters could not pay rent, so landowners were losing a lot of money.
- in 1845 there was an outbreak of potato blight in the Highlands. Crofters who depended on potatoes had to leave.
- although there were some examples of brutal treatment, some landowners paid for the crofters' journey to other countries believing that they would be better off. The Highland and Island Emigration Society was set up in 1852 to organise this.
- in 1886 the Crofters' Holding Act tried to improve crofters' lives by guaranteeing fair rents, fixed tenure and freedom of children's inheritance. This was designed to stop unfair evictions of Highlanders, but 60 000 more left between 1881 and 1931.

Quick Test

1. What was a crofter?

2. What two activities replaced farming by crofters in the Highlands?

3. How did the balance of the population between the Highlands and towns and cities change between the middle of the nineteenth century and the middle of the twentieth century?

4. Choose one piece of evidence that you consider to be the most important in attacking the actions of the landowners, and one which would be most useful in defending them. Think about why you made these choices.

Did you hit your target for this topic? Give yourself a mark out of ten.

Answers 1. Highlanders who lived on small farms **2.** Sheep farming and hunting **3.** The Highland population declined, the towns and cities got bigger

Coal mining

Growth and change

- Coal was in great demand in the nineteenth century because of the growth of the iron and steel industries, the railways, steam power and the use of gas in growing towns and cities.
- The British coal industry declined after the First World War because of competition from Germany and the USA, and the development of electricity and oil as alternatives. British coal mines were slow to adopt some of the new technologies.
- Because of technological changes, coal production increased fourteenfold between the 1830s and 1930s.
- New pits were opened that were dug deeper than ever before.

Top Tip
Try making a mind map to organise your understanding of technological change and its effects.

Coal mining involved the following:
- 'hewers' cut coal with a hand pick
- 'bearers' carrying coal in baskets up ladders on their backs
- 'drawers' pulled coal in small trucks
- 'trappers' were boys who opened trap doors to ventilate the shafts
- ponies pulled trucks of coal on iron rails
- 'stoups' were piles of coal used to hold up the roof of mine shafts
- wooden or iron props to hold up the shaft of the pit
- steam driven pumps drained deep mines of water
- steam powered ventilation systems
- steam driven winding apparatus would lift a cage carrying miners or coal up and down the shaft on wires.
- mechanical cutting equipment

Dangers of mining

Technological change had two main effects on miners' safety. By making deeper mining possible it made mining more dangerous; but technology could also reduce the dangers:

- The **Davy Lamp** in the 1830s, then electricity in the 1880s made fires less likely.
- **Ventilation fans** improved air quality from the 1860s.
- The introduction of iron cages and pit ponies reduced the dangers to workers hauling coal up wooden ladders.
- By 1900 more powerful **engines** had replaced the old steam pumps to prevent flooding.
- Metal pit props in the second half of the nineteenth century made tunnel collapses less common.

Accidents continued to be common. In 1909, 160 miners were killed when the West Stanley mine in the north east of England collapsed. 59 of those killed were under 20 years of age and there was very little compensation for families. Despite technological advances, coal mining remained hard for both miners and for surface workers. The sorting of coal was still done by hand well into the twentieth century. By 1930 there had been great technological advances in coal mining. However, British owners, having invested earlier and in older technologies than their competitors abroad, were slow to respond to these advances. For example, mechanised cutting equipment had been adopted quickly by Britain's rivals in Germany and America and Britain had fallen behind. Scottish owners had been quicker to adopt new technologies than mine owners in the rest of Britain.

Quick Test

1. Why was there an increased demand for coal in the nineteenth century?

2. What new technologies changed coal mines?

3. How did new technologies make mining more dangerous?

4. How could they help make mining safer?

Did you hit your target for this topic? Give yourself a mark out of ten.

Answers 1. The growth of iron and steel industries, of railways, steam and gas lighting **2.** Mechanisation, metal props, steam pumps, ventilation fans **3.** It made deeper mining possible **4.** Tunnel collapses less likely, fires less likely, iron cages, less prone to flooding

Railways

The opening of the first railways in Darlington, Liverpool and Manchester led to 'railway mania' in the 1830s; a boom that transformed Britain. By the 1850s there were 8000 miles of railway tracks, and by 1870s there were 16 000 miles of tracks.

Railways transform Britain

- Railways were cheaper, faster and more comfortable than travel on the roads by horse or stagecoach.
- Canals and shipping for carrying goods declined as trains were faster and less affected by the weather. Truly national markets were created for the first time. By 1898 the railways carried ten times as much freight as canals.
- Towns on railway lines grew at the expense of those not connected.
- There was a considerable boost to engineering, for example, the iron industry used 1 million tons of coal as early as 1850.
- Fresh foods in greater variety could be brought to the towns, so people's diet improved.
- The railways provided a better postal service and more rapid communication. Standard time for the whole of Britain was introduced so train timetables could be devised. Political campaigns, such as the Anti-Corn Law League could use railways.
- The possibility of commuting to work encouraged the growth of suburbs, the expansion of cities and the rise of travelling salesmen in business.
- Seaside holiday resorts sprung up and prospered now people could travel.
- There were more jobs. The use of 'navvies' to build the railways encouraged the immigration of labourers, particularly from Ireland.

Top Tip
There were both benefits and problems with the growth of the railways. Make two lists in columns to summarise these.

Government and the growth of the railways

The government encouraged the growth of railways, despite the fears and objections of canal owners, landowners, environmentalists and coach companies. They also moved to regulate and control the railways:

- Railway companies were forced to offer cheaper tickets.
- The Railway Clearing House standardised rail width (**gauge**) at 4 ft 8.5 inches (1.4 metres) so that the same trains could now run all over Britain.
- In the 1890s railway companies were forced to improve braking and signalling to improve safety after some fatal accidents.

- During the First World War the government took over all the different railway companies to make them run better. After the war (in 1921) they were **de-nationalised** (given back to private owners), but split into just four companies to make things work more efficiently. These companies found it difficult to restore the railways after the war. They also had restrictions on how much they could charge customers in each region; this made it difficult to compete.

Railways were under increasing pressure as key customers like iron and steel faced competition from abroad, and there was some competition from improved roads, cars and lorries from the 1920s onwards.

Technological improvements

- Machine cutting tools for tunnels.
- More comfortable carriages.
- Building of new bridges,
  e.g. Tay Bridge and Forth Bridge.
- Faster steam trains,
  e.g. The Mallard in 1938 reached speeds up to 126 mph.

Quick Test

1. Name three ways in which the growth of railways helped other industries grow.
2. What did the government do to make sure that there was a nationwide rail network?
3. How did the government try to make rail travel safer?
4. Why did the railways do less well from the 1920s?

Did you hit your target for this topic? Give yourself a mark out of ten.

Answers 1. Engineering and iron industries to build the railways; coal to supply fuel also; food could be transported freshly to towns; postal service was quicker and grew rapidly; holiday resorts could be reached more easily. **2.** They standardised the gauge of the tracks **3.** Braking and signalling were improved. **4.** They had difficulty getting started again after the war; clients in the iron and engineering industries had problems from foreign competition; cars and lorries on the roads were competition for them

Employment and working conditions

Working in the coal mines

You have already learned that there were many significant changes made to the technology involved in coal mining during the nineteenth century. Despite this, the key feature of working in coal mining throughout this period was that it was dangerous.

Fatal accidents were quite common. They were caused by:

- gas explosions
- flooding
- mineshafts collapsing through subsidence or poor maintenance
- ropes and cables breaking
- the use of gelignite to blast coal or new shafts
- lack of protective clothing such as helmets.

In addition miners had to put up with intense heat, rats and working in confined spaces.

In 1830 miners were better paid than most workers, but had no insurance to fall back on in the (likely) event that they were injured or if they were **laid off** (sacked from their jobs) when demand for coal fell. It was also common for whole families, men, women and children to work in the pits. A combination of government action and **trade unions** helped to change the situation.

- The **Mines Act 1842** followed a report by the **Royal Commission** that stated that children were working 14 hour days, sitting in darkness all day, were regularly beaten and were required to carry 50 kg bags. The Act forbade women and boys under 10 from working underground, and inspectors were employed to enforce the new law.

- In the 1860s and 1870s mineshafts that were particularly dangerous were outlawed and higher standards of training demanded of managers.

- In 1909 the Liberal Government introduced a maximum **8 hour day**.

Hundreds of thousands of accidents still happened each year, despite these changes, many involving children.

- From 1889 miners fought for better conditions and wages. There was a wave of strikes, from 1911 to 1914, demanding better wages and conditions. After the First World War mine owners found it increasingly difficult to compete with foreign competition. They tried to reduce wages in 1926, leading to a long **strike** which ended in failure for the miners. In the Depression that followed in the 1930s thousands lost their jobs.

Top Tip

Remember that the key thing that you are examining here is change. Note the differences in working conditions at the start, the middle and the end of the period.

Top Tip

It is important when revising to keep thinking and not 'switch off'. Rather than just reading through the key facts that you need to know, note down the main points to keep you on your toes.

Working on the land

The 1830s marked the beginning of a period of rapid change in farming as the **Enclosure** movement of the previous 100 years had replaced the old strip farming with enclosed farms that could quickly adopt new technologies. People were also being attracted to the wealth of the cities and so the number of people employed in agriculture in 1830 rapidly declined.

- There were improvements in drainage and new kinds of fertilisers, such as **guano** and '**superphosphates**'.
- Steam engines were increasingly used for ploughing and threshing amongst other things.
- From 1914 motor transport, in particular tractors, were being introduced.
- New machinery drove down wages and led to unemployment.
- The new machines caused an increase in accidents.
- Wages remained very low, accommodation was poor, and trade unions were very slow to develop and made little impact.

All of this was true, not only when agriculture was doing badly, but even during the so-called '**Golden Age of Farming**', from the 1830s to the 1880s, before cheap foreign imports from countries such as the USA led to much of Britain's food being imported and harder times for farmers and their labourers. At the end of the Golden Age there was an agricultural depression during which employment in the countryside fell by a quarter.

Quick Test

1. What were the main causes of fatal accidents amongst mineworkers?

2. What practices in the mines did governments intervene to improve?

3. What new machinery was introduced into the countryside?

4. How did these new machines change agricultural work in the countryside?

Did you hit your target for this topic? Give yourself a mark out of ten.

Answers 1. Gas explosions; flooding; mineshafts collapsing; ropes and cables breaking; the use of gelignite **2.** Children working; length of the working day; dangerous types of mines **3.** Steam engines and tractors **4.** There were more accidents and increased unemployment

Health and housing in the countryside

Health

By modern standards the health of people in the countryside was poor in the 1830s.

- In 1842, the **Chadwick Report**, a government report into the conditions of people in Britain carried out by a man called Edwin Chadwick, suggested that the life expectancy of a labourer in the countryside was 38, while that of a member of the land-owning classes was 52.
- The working hours for people in the countryside were long, their houses were damp and their diet lacked variety and vitamins.
- Most people found doctors' fees unaffordable.

However, compared to people living in towns and cities at the time, country dwellers were comparatively healthy. Chadwick found that life expectancy for town workers was less than half of that of country labourers. The reasons for this were because in the countryside:

- there was less overcrowding, so diseases did not spread so quickly
- water was less likely to be contaminated
- sanitation was shared with fewer people
- as time passed people in the country could benefit from transport to hospitals in the towns and from new medical discoveries.

Housing

For most, accommodation was very basic in 1830.

- Single migrant labourers lived in bothies (shared single room stone shelters).
- Families who worked as labourers lived in one or two roomed 'blackhouses' made from stone, wood and turf with earth floors trampled down. Lacking chimneys, they were smoky and the thatch was liable to rot. They shared accommodation with animals.
- Seasonally, in more remote areas they might stay in 'shielings', even simpler often beehive-shaped dwellings in mountain areas.
- Some cottages were 'tied' (a part of the pay and conditions for the job). This meant that when times were hard and labourers were laid off, their home was also lost.
- Miners' cottages were often in better condition, but tended to be overcrowded.
- Farmers often lived in much more comfortable accommodation, well furnished on two floors, while the big landowners could live in very large houses, staffed by a large number of servants and surrounded by extensive gardens.

From the 1850s, many landlords made improvements to the accommodation of their tenants, beginning with basic maintenance and strengthening outside and more furniture inside. Cottages eventually acquired baths and indoor sanitation, but these were gained much later than in towns and cities. When they arrived, these improvements meant an increase in rent which labourers could not always afford.

By contrast, other prominent features of the countryside in Scotland were the castles of the wealthy landowners and comfortable two-storey farmhouses of better off farmers. As the Clearances made way for hunting in some areas, large hunting lodges might boast ten or more bedrooms, servants and great luxury. These lodges could also provide new types of employment and sometimes accommodation for local people.

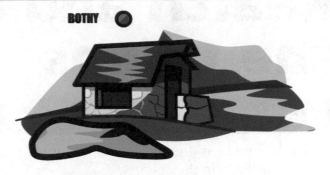

BOTHY

BLACKHOUSE

SHIELING

Top Tip
It is often a good idea when revising to use visual triggers that are significant to you. Try drawing a mind map of rural health and housing that features little drawings of turf houses, bothies and shielings, etc. that make sense to you. These images should help you recall the information when you need it most; in the examination hall.

Quick Test

1. What were the main features of 'blackhouses'?

2. Why were improvements in accommodation not always a help to poorer workers?

3. Why was the health of people in the countryside generally better than that of people in the towns?

4. What improvements did many landlords make after the 1850's?

Did you hit your target for this topic? Give yourself a mark out of ten.

Answers 1. Labourers' families' houses made from turf, wood and stone. **2.** Their rent was increased. **3.** There was less overcrowding, so diseases did not spread so quickly; water was less likely to be contaminated; sanitation was shared with fewer people. **4.** Basic maintenance; more furniture; better sanitation

Health and housing in the towns

Health and housing in the 1830s

- By the middle of the nineteenth century as many people lived in towns and cities as lived in the country.
- There was much **overcrowding**. Families often shared a single room, new houses were hurriedly built with poor **sanitation** and poor **ventilation**. The worst areas were called **slums**.
- Water supplies were obtained from shared water pumps, there were open sewers, and drinking water was not properly separated from waste water.
- Fresh food was often mixed with non-fresh food so went bad.
- Working conditions were dangerous.
- There was little support for the poor, sick and old. People were desperate to stay out of the **poorhouses** (created in 1834 by the Poor Law Amendment Act).
- Major **epidemics** (outbreaks of diseases such as tuberculosis, typhus, typhoid, smallpox, scarlet fever and cholera) killed thousands. Tuberculosis was the biggest killer of all and it affected all classes. Cholera and typhoid were particularly linked to poor sanitation, with major outbreaks in 1831; 1848; 1853 and 1866.

Government intervention

- At first the government favoured a policy of **laissez-faire** (leave things be).
- A better understanding of diseases led to action being taken gradually. Dr John Snow linked the cholera epidemic in 1831 in London to contaminated water pumps. In 1842 Edwin Chadwick linked poor housing to low life expectancy. In 1883–84 Robert Koch found the germ causing cholera.
- In 1848 a **Public Health Act** allowed local councils to set up health boards and health officers to improve water supply and drains.
- In 1875 a Public Health Act forced local authorities to provide proper drainage, water supply and sewerage systems, and to maintain streets with lighting and paving to an adequate standard. Glasgow had a proper sewerage system by the 1890s.
- The **Artisans' Dwellings Act 1875** gave councils the power to pull down slums. Birmingham Council rebuilt the entire city centre.
- The Liberal Government of 1906 to 1918 introduced school meals and medical inspections for children in 1906–7 and sickness insurance for many workers in 1911.

- After the First World War, **Addison's Housing Act 1919** aimed to provide homes fit for returning soldiers, but ran out of money. **Wheatley's Housing Act 1924** was more successful, but the good quality council housing provided was too expensive for poorer workers.

Microscope

Drains

Legislation

Top Tip

To get a picture of the changes taking place here write out five of the key problems in health and housing and then put a cross through each one as something happens to reduce or eliminate it. Write beside each cross what brought about the change.

Health and housing in the 1930s

- By the 1930s towns had sewerage systems, reservoirs, bathhouses, water pipes and electricity. Multi-room houses with indoor toilets were the norm. Cholera had been wiped out, TB halved and typhoid reduced due to better sanitation and better diet. Smallpox had also been wiped out by vaccination.

- The railways meant that fresher and more varied food supplies were available, as well as soap, cheap cotton clothing, and medicines for hospitals.

- Wages had risen, and there was the beginning of a government 'safety net' for the poor and sick.

Quick Test

1. What is meant by the term laissez-faire?

2. What caused major epidemics of cholera and typhoid in British cities in this period?

3. Why was life expectancy in the cities worse than in the countryside?

4. Find five key reasons for the improvements in health and housing that took place in these years.

Did you hit your target for this topic? Give yourself a mark out of ten.

Answers 1. Leave things be **2.** Overcrowding and poor sanitation **3.** There was overcrowding and it took time before proper sanitation was provided **4.** Local governments built better sanitation; government Health Acts; better medical knowledge; Addison's and Wheatley's Housing Acts; better food thanks to railways; vaccination; safety net for the poor

Political representation

Government in the 1800s

In the early 1800s the British Government was run by ministers chosen from Parliament (the House of Lords or the House of Commons). Lords were not elected and the system for electing the MPs in the House of Commons had grown up over hundreds of years and in ways that seemed, to many people, to be unfair.

- Only a limited number of people had the vote (a **restricted franchise**).
- Who could vote depended on what property they owned.
- Changes in the population of Britain meant that the new towns and cities were not well represented.
- Bribery and corruption were rife.

Great Reform Act 1832

There was a long campaign for **reform** of the voting system for the House of Commons by 'radicals'. Eventually, the Whig Party (wealthy landowners) passed the **1832 Reform Act** against the opposition of the Tories (also gentry).

- The **franchise** (the vote) was given to middle class people, defined as the '£10 Householder', increasing the electorate by around 200 000 to 652 000.
- The worst examples of **rotten boroughs** (constituencies where very few, or in one or two cases, no people lived) were abolished.
- 90% of the population still had no vote and constituencies were very uneven in size.

The biggest impact of the 'Great Reform Act' was that it showed that reform was possible.

One of the immediate effects of the Great Reform Act was to encourage 'radicals' to seek a further extension of the vote to the Working Class. The most significant campaign for the vote was the **Chartist** movement, based in the north of England. The Chartists supported the implementation of 6 points of the '**People's Charter**', including universal male suffrage (votes for all adult men), vote by ballot, more equal constituencies, payment of MPs and the abolition of property qualifications. All but one of their demands (a demand for annual elections) came to pass. However, divisions between those advocating physical force and those supporting peaceful methods, combined with stubborn suppression by the government, had defeated the Chartists by the end of 1848. It was only once this danger was long past that Parliament began to contemplate extending the vote to the working class.

Top Tip
There are a lot of details involved in the main Acts in this section. Try drawing three or four cartoons to show how each measure or set of measures increased the franchise, made constituencies fairer and tackled corruption.

Second Reform Act 1867 (1868 in Scotland)

The new Liberal Party, led by William Gladstone and Lord Russell in 1866, believed that honest, self improving and thoughtful members of the working class should get the vote. They attempted to pass a new reform act. Whigs in the Liberal Party rebelled and Gladstone's measure was defeated.

The Conservative Party, led by Lord Derby and Benjamin Disraeli, wanted to humiliate Gladstone and, believing that more reform was now inevitable anyway, passed their own Act in 1867 that gave the vote to many more working class voters.

All male householders over 21 living in towns (boroughs) were given the vote. This meant there were 1 200 000 new voters.

This changed politics because now politicians had to make popular appeals. This was too big an electorate to easily control.

Continuing reform in the 1800s

- 1872: The **Secret Ballot Act** introduced voting in secret, and made bribery a waste of time.
- 1883: The **Corrupt and Illegal Practices Act** gave prison sentences for corruption.
- 1884: The **Third Reform Act** meant that all male householders, lodgers and tenants resident for at least one year in a house worth more than £10 could vote. This meant that a lot of men working in the countryside were given the vote.
- 1885: The **Redistribution of Seats Act** made constituencies more equal in size.
- Political Parties had to become more organised to attract support from all classes.
- In 1900 the Labour Party was founded, specifically to represent the interests of working people.

Quick Test

1. Why was the unreformed voting system unfair?
2. What was important about the Great Reform Act?
3. How many people were able to vote following the Second Reform Act?
4. In what ways did the voting system become fairer and less corrupt as the 1800s went on?

Did you hit your target for this topic? Give yourself a mark out of ten.

Answers 1. Many new towns and cities were not properly represented; the right to vote depended on what property you owned; most people could not vote including all women. **2.** It showed that reform was possible. **3.** Almost 2 million. **4.** Bribery and intimidation were outlawed; parts of the country, especially towns and cities, had a greater share of representation than before; a greater number of people could vote; political parties developed to channel representation in government

Women and the vote

The position of women in 1830

Women of all classes were treated as second class citizens in early Victorian Britain.

- Women had no right to take part in the political process as voters, councillors or Members of Parliament. The middle class ideal was that a woman should be 'the angel of the house'.

- A lack of political rights made it harder for women to fight for other aims, such as improving their rights within marriage or their rights to own property. Access to education was also very limited and, even for wealthy girls, education was designed to prepare them to be good wives and mothers.

Campaigning for the vote

- The first movement set up by women to fight for votes, or **suffrage** for women, was the **Suffragist movement** (National Union of Women's Suffrage Societies – NUWSS). This was founded by Millicent Fawcett in 1887.

- The Suffragists hoped to persuade MPs and other influential men that women were ready and had the right to take part in the political process. They did this by acting peacefully, campaigning through leaflets, discussion meetings and letter writing. This was effective in persuading around half of MPs to support the idea of votes for women by 1914.

- Some women grew impatient with the Suffragists' methods. The issue of the vote for women was raised 15 times in Parliament and was always rejected. In 1903 Emmeline Pankhurst founded the Women's Social and Political Union (WSPU), nicknamed the **Suffragettes**. Together with her daughters, Christabel and Sylvia, she wanted to take more direct and **militant** action to win the vote.

- The Suffragettes disrupted political meetings held by MPs, dug up golf courses, fire bombed cricket pavilions, broke windows, sent fire bombs to politicians and chained themselves to railings. When arrested, some Suffragettes went on hunger strike. The most famous incident involved a Suffragette called **Emily Davison**, who died trying to stop the King's horse during the 1913 Epsom Derby horse race.

- In Scotland the Suffragettes were a part of the Federation of Scottish Suffrage Societies and their actions included burning down Whitekirk Church, Ayr Racecourse and Leuchars railway station.

The First World War was a key turning point in women obtaining the vote. Women took over jobs in factories and driving ambulances when men went to war, showing that they had an important contribution to make to the war effort, particularly in munitions work.

The **Representation of the People Act 1918** for the first time gave women over 30 the right to vote and become MPs, and gave the vote to the remaining 40 per cent of men who could not vote. In 1928 women over 21 were finally given the vote on the same basis as men.

Top Tip
The Suffragettes made the most obvious impact in the fight for votes for women. However, many would argue that the more peaceful methods of the Suffragists and the First World War played greater roles in winning votes for women.

Government response

- The Liberal Prime Minister Asquith was against votes for women. He thought that women would be more likely to vote Conservative.
- The Suffragettes in prison who went on hunger strike from 1909 were force fed. In response to outrage at the cruelty involved in this practice, in 1913 the government passed the **Temporary Discharge Act**, nicknamed the **Cat and Mouse Act**, because it allowed hunger striking women to be released until they recovered. They were then rearrested without the need for a new trial.
- Government militancy won more sympathy for the cause of women's suffrage from some people, but Suffragette militancy hardened the attitudes of many MPs and the government.

CREDIT

Quick Test

1. What methods did the Suffragists use to try to win the vote?

2. How did the Suffragettes try to speed up the process?

3. Why might the First World War be described as a turning point in the campaign for votes for women?

4. When did women win the vote on the same basis as men?

Did you hit your target for this topic? Give yourself a mark out of ten.

Answers 1. Peaceful persuasion – they campaigned using leaflets, discussion meetings and letter writing. **2.** They used more active, militant and sometimes violent methods **3.** It gave women a chance to clearly show their contribution to national life. **4.** 1928

Enquiry skills

Below are two sources and some questions that you might be asked in the Enquiry skills section of the exam paper.
You will first be given an issue:

A better diet during the nineteenth century resulted in an increase in the population.

There will then be three questions for you to answer. The first will ask you how useful one of the sources would be to you in addressing the issue in the box. The second will ask you what evidence supports or argues against the issue. The third will asks you how far you agree with the issue.
When tackling 'Enquiry skills' in the examination, don't be afraid to write on the exam paper. Annotations, underlining and/or highlighting key words and phrases really help you to focus on the content of the source and the needs of the question that you have been asked.

Top Tip
Make sure you read the questions first so that you know what to look for in the sources. When tackling Enquiry skills questions in the examination, do not be afraid to write on the exam paper. Annotations, underlining and/or highlighting key words and phrases really help you to focus on the content of the source and the question that you have been asked.

Source A was written by Elizabeth Dowling in 1900. It gives her memories of growing up in Central Scotland.

I remember when I was young seeing new shops being opened up in our town. There were grocers' shops that sold vegetables brought in fresh by the railways from the country. Bakers sold bread and pastries and my family could afford to buy fresh meat from the butcher every week. People now seem to live longer and have larger families than before.

Source B is from *The Social History of Britain*, by Anthony S Dorian, written in 1990.

In towns across Britain local authorities worked to improve the conditions that people lived in, improving housing and hygiene, for example, through building sewerage systems. More children survived and healthier parents gave birth to more and healthier babies. It was this decrease in the rate of infant mortality that explains the drop in death rate in Britain.

1. How useful is Source A for investigating causes of population growth in Scotland during the nineteenth century? 4 marks

You might answer this question like this:

This source is useful in showing how diet improved health and encouraged population growth in Scotland, although it is a little limited because it is only one account. Because it was written at the time by someone who saw how towns and diets changed for the better in the nineteenth century first hand, it is very useful and tells us a lot. The growth of the railways helped to bring fresh food quickly into towns so better quality food that was cheap enough for most families to buy meant that larger families could be sustained. One drawback is that it only shows an experience in central Scotland and not other parts of Scotland, such as the Highlands where the population was falling.

- Note that the candidate has often put the answer into her or his own words rather than copying out large amounts.
- The candidate has clearly stated how useful the source is in relation to the question.
- Note that, where it helps, the candidate has used some recalled knowledge to add to the answer, showing what has been left out.

Top Tip

For 'how useful' questions it is often a good idea to have a routine to help you focus and develop your answer. For example, Who wrote this and why? How do they get their ideas across? Are there any key facts left out?

Now tackle the other two questions:

2. What evidence in Source A supports the view that a better diet led to an increase in the population? What evidence in Source B reveals other reasons for an increase in the population?   4 marks

3. How far do you agree that a better diet led to the growth of population in nineteenth century Scotland? You must use evidence from the sources and your own knowledge to come to a conclusion.   5 marks

State clearly whether you agree or disagree, for example:

"I agree that, although not the only factor, the changes in diet in nineteenth century Scotland was the most important reason for the increasing population."

First use information in the sources and then use your own 'recalled' information that the sources have not included to support your answer. For example:

"Source A highlights that changes in transport such as the railways and shipping allowed a greater variety of foods to be eaten by people in cities and this food was much fresher than before. In particular, meat and fresh fruit and vegetables made people healthier and better able to resist disease. It also enabled people to have larger families, both because healthier mothers could bear children over a longer period and because it was possible to feed a larger family. As source B suggests, this was also due to improvements in housing and hygiene, but diet played the greater role."

Population and migration

Population

The populations of Scotland and Britain as a whole rose dramatically between 1880 and 2001.

- In Britain it rose from 29.7 million to 58.7 million.
- In Scotland it rose from 3.7 million to 5.5 million.

Whereas before this period population increase could be attributed mainly to a rise in the birth rate, in the last 120 years the birth rate has steadily fallen. Between the 1880s and 2000 the average British family decreased in size by two thirds.

The increasing population in this period is primarily explained by the falling death rate. The death rate in Britain has halved since the 1870s, when the death rate ran at over 20 per thousand, while life expectancy has increased by almost 80 per cent. The reasons for this are as follows:

- Better and more varied diet; cheap imports of meat, cereals and fruit.
- Decline in child labour.
- Improvements in welfare provision such as pensions, sickness and unemployment benefits.
- The **National Health Service**, providing free medical care for all.
- Medical advances, for example in antibiotics and vaccines.
- Housing and sanitation improvements, for example, clean water, affordable fuel, washing and laundry facilities.

Top Tip
Much of the information for this section overlaps with that on population and migration in Unit IB.

Migration

- Irish immigration had been a major factor in life in Britain in the nineteenth century and this continued into the twentieth century, but at a reduced rate.
- Italian immigration from the poorer parts of southern Italy led to around 4000 Italians settling in Scotland early in the twentieth century, with a further 20 000 coming from Russia and the Baltic states such as Lithuania. Some were looking for work, others escaping persecution.
- From the 1950s onwards the government encouraged people to immigrate to Britain from around the **Commonwealth**, particularly Asia and the Caribbean, to make up for shortages in some areas of employment. Most of these immigrants settled in England, particularly the prosperous south, but a significant number of Asian immigrants also settled in central Scotland.

During the twentieth century there has been a lot of emigration from Scotland:

- While the **Crofters' Holding Act 1886** gave some relief to the Highland crofters who had suffered most in the Clearances, the de-population of the Highlands continued and the highest proportion of emigrants came from these areas.
- Around half went to the USA, the other half to Canada, New Zealand and South Africa.
- In the years just before the First World War, 600 000 Scots emigrated.
- Patterns of emigration were closely linked to times when the economy was doing poorly, except for the 1930s when the whole world suffered a Depression so that there was nothing to be gained from emigrating.

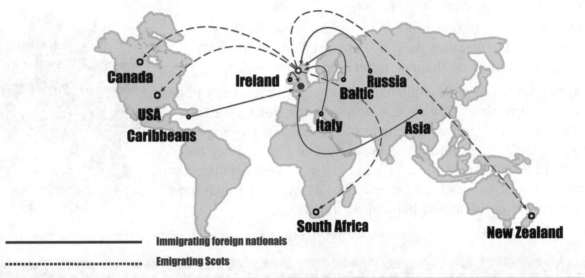

———————————————— Immigrating foreign nationals

·· Emigrating Scots

Towns and cities

Urbanisation continued throughout the twentieth century, with only 20 per cent of the population not living in large urban centres by 2000, and only 2 per cent working in agriculture. The reasons for this included:

- increased mechanisation on farms
- more employment opportunities in towns and cities
- the appeal of facilities and culture of towns and cities.

CREDIT

Quick Test

1. By how much did the population of Britain increase between 1880 and 2001?
2. What has been the most significant factor in the growth of the population of Britain since 1880?
3. What has played the greater role in patterns of migration in Scotland, immigration or emigration?
4. Why have people continued to move to towns and cities in the last 100 years?

Did you hit your target for this topic? Give yourself a mark out of ten.

Answers 1. By 21.7 million **2.** The falling death rate **3.** Both have been important, but the numbers emigrating have been larger. **4.** Mechanisation; employment opportunities; the appeal of facilities and culture of towns and cities

Shipbuilding

Changes in shipbuilding

From the beginning of the twentieth century there were major changes in shipbuilding:

- Iron then steel ships replaced wooden ships, so shipbuilding industries relocated to iron and coal deposits.
- Steam ships replaced sailing ships, and these got faster, thanks to Parson's steam turbine.
- Ships got larger and could travel further than before.
- More machine tools were used, powered by electricity.
- In the 1960s it became possible to use enclosed yards that were less subject to the weather. Assembly line **prefabricated** methods allowed the building of cheaper, larger ships more quickly.

Different kinds of ships were in demand at different times. Early in the period cargo ships for trading were most important. Before the First World War great prestige was attached to large and fast passenger liners such as the *Oceanic* and (most famously) the *Titanic*. Since the Second World War massive oil tankers and ferries have been important sources of shipbuilding work. In the years before the First and Second World Wars naval building was particularly important.

Top Tip
Make a mind map to organise your understanding of technological change and its effects on shipbuilding.

The fortunes of British shipbuilders

From the 1880s to the early 1920s, Britain's dominant trading position gave British shipbuilding the pre-eminent place in the world, with 80 per cent of the world's ships built in British shipyards in the 1890s (this had reduced to 60 per cent by 1914). Scotland was especially well placed to take advantage of this due to:

- deep rivers that were protected from the weather
- easy access to steel producers
- a plentiful and skilled workforce
- engineering expertise.

20 per cent of the world's ships were built in Scotland from 1906–14, primarily on the Clyde.

The pre-war naval race from 1906 to 1914, and then the need to replace shipping after the First World War meant that British shipbuilding remained prosperous until the early 1920s.

During the 1920s orders declined sharply and after the Wall Street Crash of 1929 things got even worse. Increased foreign competition from, often government **subsidised**, yards in Germany and Japan combined with less demand for naval building resulted in thousands of shipyard workers losing their jobs. Some yards, such as Palmer's of Jarrow closed completely.

There was some revival thanks to rearmament in the late 1930s and rebuilding after the Second World War, but from the 1950s British shipbuilding went into a longer term decline:

- There was a general slump in orders worldwide until the 1960s.
- There was increased foreign competition from the USA, Germany, Japan, Scandinavia and Korea, They were using the latest technology and cheaper labour. British shipbuilders were slow to innovate, leading to higher costs and failure to meet deadlines.
- British shipyards were less subsidised than foreign competitors, even after the British shipyards were **nationalised** in 1977.
- Industrial relations were poor. Management blamed restrictive practices, such as the strict **demarcation** of jobs between workers for failure, while unions blamed poor management for the failure to attract new orders.
- By the mid 1980s only around 2 per cent of the world's ships were built in Britain.

NEW METHODS	OLD TECHNOLOGY
NEW SHIPYARDS	OLD SHIPYARDS
NEW TECHNOLOGY	RESTRICTIVE PRACTICES
GOVERNMENT SUBSIDIES	POOR MANAGEMENT
ON TIME	SMALL SUBSIDIES
QUICK	LATE
CHEAP	EXPENSIVE
MORE ORDERS	FEW ORDERS

The decline of British shipbuilding was caused by many factors.

Quick Test

1. What were the main technological changes in shipbuilding in the twentieth century?

2. Why was shipbuilding particularly strong in Scotland?

3. What was the impact of the First and Second World Wars on shipbuilding?

4. Why did British shipbuilding continue to decline in the 1960s and 1970s when other countries' shipbuilding recovered?

Did you hit your target for this topic? Give yourself a mark out of ten.

Answers 1. The development of iron and steel ships; steam power; electrical machine tools; prefabrication **2.** Deep rivers; steel production; skilled workforce; engineering expertise **3.** It gave it a boost **4.** British shipyards had fewer subsidies; slower to innovate; poor industrial relations

The motor car

Mass production

Until the First World War cars were relatively rare and only for the rich. In the early 1900s Henry Ford in the USA introduced a new technique for building cars, called an **assembly line**, which allowed for the **mass production** of cheap motor cars, beginning with the Model T.

- Each worker in the factory did just one job on each car that passed by on the assembly line, e.g. fitting the headlights. This process was also called **Taylorism**; and although it could be dull and repetitive, Ford car workers were more highly paid than other workers.

- These ideas were copied, not only for car making, but also for lorries and electrical goods.

- The middle classes could now afford cars. The first British mass produced car was the **Morris Cowley**, made in Oxford. 445 000 cars were produced in Britain in 1938.

The impact of the car

- Houses and streets changed: houses had garages; streets were wider to allow parking and travel by car; petrol stations appeared to supply fuel.

- Trams and buses became common from the 1920s and 1930s. This provided greater freedom of travel for all classes of people because it was cheap.

- Accidents were caused by the increasing numbers of cars on the roads. This led to government action. Speed limits were imposed: 12 mph in 1896, 20 mph in 1904, 30 mph in 1935. Traffic lights were introduced in 1926, a driving test, zebra crossings and **Belisha Beacons** were introduced in 1934.

- After the Second World War one way traffic systems, pedestrian precincts and motorways became new features of the town and country; anti-drink driving laws, safety campaigns and compulsory seatbelt use are more recent innovations.

- The centres of 'light industry' such as car building took over from the 'heavy industries' of the North, and so the centres of wealth moved to the English Midlands and South. However, from the 1960s and 1970s foreign competition from Japan, Germany, France and Italy, poor management, poor quality and the reputation of the British car industry for poor labour relations led to a decline in British production. Imports increased from 1568 in 1950 to 863 000 cars in 1980.
- Following the **Beeching Report**, much of the railway system was dismantled in the 1960s.

Top Tip

Use the Internet, library or other resources to see what other benefits and drawbacks that you can find with heavy motor car use in the twentieth century.

Benefits and problems of increased car use

CREDIT

Benefits

- People could travel where they wanted.
- They brought remote areas within reach.
- There was greater scope for commuting.
- Technological improvements since 1945 made cars more economical and safer.
- Goods could be delivered to customers' doorsteps.

Problems

- The number of cars on Britain's roads increased from just over 1.5 million in 1945 to almost 23 million by 1997.
- Traffic jams were very common; road accidents were frequent and often fatal.
- Pollution: lead and other harmful substances are given off by car and lorry exhausts, caused public health problems and damage to old buildings.
- Road repairs were constantly required as roads were not built to sustain such heavy use.
- Road building caused environmental damage.

Quick Test

1. What new method of manufacturing was introduced by Henry Ford in the USA?

2. How did the motor car change British towns?

3. What was the impact of the Beeching report?

4. What have been the main benefits and problems of the rise of the motor car?

Did you hit your target for this topic? Give yourself a mark out of ten.

Answers 1. Assembly line production **2.** Wider streets; garages and petrol stations appeared; speed limits in town centres; traffic lights; pedestrian precincts; zebra crossings; railway lines closed down **3.** Thousands of railway lines were closed. **4. Benefits:** Flexibility to go where you want; remote areas within reach; commuting and variety of work; more economical and safer; increased choice; delivery of goods to customers' doorsteps **Problems:** Traffic jams; road accidents; pollution, causing public health problems and damage to old buildings; roads and bridges could not sustain such heavy use; environmental damage; large lorries come into towns

Women at work

Women at work before 1945

At the beginning of the twentieth century 2 million women in Britain worked outside the home. There were two types of work in which women were most likely to be engaged:

- **Domestic service**, such as maids, housekeepers, cooks and governesses. The hours were long, with 14 hour days being common.

- **Sweated labour**, such as seamstresses, matchmaking, brick making and chain making. This was heavy manual labour, and was very poorly paid. Matchmakers were paid 20p per day, and they often became ill due to phosphorous poisoning.

There were campaigns by women such as Annie Besant to improve the conditions of working women, and the Campaign for Women's Suffrage was partly aimed at enabling women to improve their employment.

Education Acts in 1875, 1902 and 1918 opened up new possibilities. Women were allowed to become doctors and teachers, but were not paid the same as men, and female teachers had to resign when they married. 65 per cent of teachers in Scotland were women by 1914.

The growth of light industries, the typewriter, and a growth in banking created more new opportunities, such as assembly line work, secretarial and clerical work.

The First World War briefly allowed 1 million women to do new kinds of work, such as drive trams, and their pay increased significantly during the war. Most had to resign when conscription ended and the men returned from the Front. The **1919 Sex Disqualification Act** created more openings for women in universities.

Top Tip

It is worth noting that sometimes the position of women in the workplace got better and at other times things got worse. A useful way of making this clear might be to make a graph showing ups and downs of women at work.

Women at work since 1945

Women played an even larger part in both the armed forces and in working to support the war effort in the Second World War than in the First. After the Second World War there was continued demand for women at work, so changes were more lasting.

- During the war restrictions on married women working ended and nurseries were set up.
- By 1957 29 per cent of married women were in paid work.
- From the 1960s there was a renewed campaign by women to raise public awareness of the inequalities faced by women in Britain.
- Equal pay was introduced first into the Civil Service in the mid-1950s, then in 1969 the **Equal Pay Act** made it officially illegal to pay a women less than a man for doing the same job. A new Equal Pay Act was still needed in 1984, however, to define equality on the basis of work of equal value.
- The **1975 Sex Discrimination Act** intended to provide equality when appointments for jobs were made. However, men are still paid more than women on average in the workplace, and men are more prevalent than women in the best paid professions.

Quick Test

1. What jobs were open to most women in the 1880s?

2. How and why did the variety of jobs available improve in the 1920s and 1930s?

3. What was the impact of the Second World War on women's opportunities in the workplace?

4. How did government action attempt to improve the inequality faced by women?

Did you hit your target for this topic? Give yourself a mark out of ten.

Answers 1. Domestic service or sweated labour. **2.** Educational opportunities improved: technologies such as the typewriter and light industry provided new opportunities; World War One provided new experiences. **3.** Women were given a taste of independence, but many had to give up jobs immediately after the war. **4.** The Sex Disqualification Act 1919 opened opportunities in education; the Equal Pay Act and Sex Discrimination Acts attempted to create a more equal environment in the workplace

Trade unions

The changing influence of the trade unions

- Before the 1880s only skilled workers had unions, called craft unions, to preserve their better pay and status.

- From the 1880s new unions were larger and included unskilled workers. The good organisation and peaceful approach taken by these unions impressed many and led to the formation of similar unions of labourers and textile workers.

- Union membership grew from a little over 500 000 in 1880 to 6 million in 1938, to a peak at over 12 million in 1977.

- Trade union rights were improved through legislation after 1906, through the influence of Labour MPs.

- The power of the unions brought them into conflict with governments during the prosperous years of the 1970s. In the 1980s, however, the Conservative Government passed legislation to reduce union power. The **1980 Employment Act** made 'secondary picketing' (picketing by those not on strike) illegal, and the **1984 Employment Act** forced unions to hold a secret ballot before any strike action could be taken.

- By the end of the 1980s union membership was only two thirds what it had been at the start of the decade and its membership continued to fall.

- From the 1990s the role of trade unions returned to a large extent to what it had been at the time of the craft unions, providing insurance and other limited benefits to their members.

Industrial action

Although there are many kinds of action that unions could take to get employers to improve conditions for union members, the most effective action, particularly for unskilled workers, was the withdrawal of labour through a **strike**. There were many important examples of strikes during the late nineteenth and twentieth centuries:

- The **Match Girls strike 1888** led to improved conditions for women employees of Bryant and May.

- **The Dockers Strike 1889** led to slightly better pay and job security for dockers. It showed that large scale strikes could work and need not be violent.

- The **1926 General Strike** was a result of mine owners trying to cut miners' wages. Tough government action broke the general strike in 10 days and the miners were defeated.

Trade unions played an important role in ensuring that increasing prosperity from the 1950s was reflected in the pay and living standards of workers.

- Inflation led governments to try to impose wage restraint. Trade unions fought this and, in 1974, succeeded in bringing down the government of Edward Heath.

- The Conservative Government of the 1980s was able to take advantage of rising unemployment to take on the unions through legislation that made striking more difficult. In the biggest confrontation between trade unions and the government in 1984–85, the miners' union (the NUM) was defeated.

Top Tip

When times were good economically, unions were able to win improved pay and conditions for their members through actual or threatened industrial action. However, when there was the threat of unemployment, unions were weak as uncertainty over their jobs made members reluctant to strike.

The Labour Party

To defend their right to exist and defend the interests of their members, the new unions set up their own political party in 1900 – the Labour Party. Many Labour MPs were directly sponsored by trade unions and, first in co-operation with the Liberals with whom the Labour Party had an electoral pact and later on their own, the Labour Party was able to defend the rights of trade unionists.

Members of trade unions paid a **political levy** to support the Labour Party. In the 1960s and 1970s, however, trade unions came into conflict with the government over the economic policies of Labour Prime Minister Harold Wilson and his successor Jim Callaghan. With the birth of '**New Labour**' in 1994, the Labour Party began to loosen its links with the trade unions, for example by reducing their ability to influence policy and elections within the party.

Quick Test

1. What was new about the new unions of the 1880s?

2. At what times were trade unions at their strongest?

3. How many workers were members of trade unions at their height in 1977?

4. What weakened the position of trade unions between the wars and in the 1980s?

Did you hit your target for this topic? Give yourself a mark out of ten.

Answers 1. They included unskilled workers. **2.** When the economy was strong and unemployment was low. **3.** 12 million **4.** Rising unemployment and government action including new legislation.

Health and housing

Health and housing in the towns

Housing in British towns was little better in 1880 than it had been in 1830, with overcrowding and poor sanitation, as well as back to back (England) and tenement (Scotland) housing predominant in the new towns and cities. However, changes brought about by the **1875 Public Health Act** were beginning to take effect, as Glasgow and other large cities improved their sewerage systems and water supplies. **Slum clearances** and housing improvement schemes were also under way, and further improvements were brought by the **Housing Acts** of Addison (1919), Wheatley (1924) and Greenwood (1930) creating better quality housing.

Top Tip
There is considerable overlap between this section and the sections 'Health and housing in the countryside' and 'Health and housing in the towns' in Unit IB.

However, the Second World War heralded some of the biggest changes in housing in Britain:

- Many of the 0.5 million slum houses remaining in 1939 were demolished by Hitler's '**blitz**' of inner cities during the war.

- It was calculated that 1.25 million new homes were needed.

- A shortage of materials created some delay in building these new homes. As a temporary measure **prefabricated** houses were built out of concrete slabs, asbestos and corrugated iron. Many residents thought they were luxurious compared to what they were used to, and they were still lived in decades later.

- There was resettlement of around 0.75 million people in large council housing schemes on the edges of major cities. These were not always well planned; they lacked leisure facilities, shops and pubs. The community spirit of tenement slums was not maintained, so that crime and vandalism led to abandoned housing.

- The **1946 New Towns Act** had created 32 New Towns by 1971, e.g. East Kilbride, Glenrothes and Livingston. This moved almost a million people out of cities. Here there was better planning, providing shopping centres, schools, community halls, pedestrian safety, play spaces and the encouragement of new industries.

- A boom in private house building since the 1970s and the encouragement of tenants to buy their council houses by the government in the 1980s led to increasing home ownership.

The biggest improvements in health in towns occurred between the 1880s and 1930s, with improvements in living standards, sanitation and medical advances eradicating many of the major dangers to public health that plagued towns in the nineteenth century. After the Second World War the single biggest improvement to public health was achieved through the foundation of the **National Health Service** (NHS) in 1948.

From the cradle to the grave.

The NHS provided free medical, dental, hospital and optical care 'from the cradle to the grave'. Its first big success was the near eradication of TB, as well as much improved dental and maternity care, and the almost universal availability of many new medical technologies such as antibiotics. However, its unexpected popularity and spiralling cost led to compromises. These include prescription charges, charges for opticians' and dentists' services, complaints about inefficiency and delays in some areas.

Health and housing in the countryside

- Council house building before and after the Second World War brought great improvements to rural housing.
- The movement to small towns and large villages from scattered settlements helped in the provision of water, electricity and other facilities.
- The health of people living in the countryside was better than those living in towns. This improved further due to changes in working patterns that reduced the amount of hard manual labour needed.

Quick Test

1. What difference did government actions make to housing in Britain in these years?

2. Give five reasons why the health of the British population improved from 1880.

3. Why were the original ideas of the National Health Service compromised?

4. Why were 'prefabs' less temporary than originally intended?

Did you hit your target for this topic? Give yourself a mark out of ten.

Answers 1. Governments were able to make a greater impact after the Second World War because of the effects of the Blitz, for example in the creation of New Towns. Some of these changes seemed to be for the better, but sometimes they made things worse – for example by destroying the community spirit of the tenements. **2.** Wealth and living standards have improved; housing and sanitation have improved; medical and scientific advances; the National Health Service was introduced. **3.** Its popularity; the cost of new treatments; an aging population. **4.** Their residents liked living in them.

Political representation and votes for women

Representation in the twentieth century

Several Acts of Parliament have served to increase the representation of British people in the last 100 years:

- **1918 Representation of the People Act** – the vote was granted to all men over 21 and all women over 30.
- **1928 Representation of the People Act** – the vote was granted to all women over 21.
- **1947 Representation of the People Act** – this removed some of the remaining anomalies in the voting system that allowed a few people two votes.
- In 1969, the voting age was lowered to 18.

Top Tip

There is considerable overlap between this section and the sections 'Political representation' and 'Women and the vote' in Unit IB.

In 1999 some of the powers of the Parliament in Westminster were devolved to a Parliament in Edinburgh and Assemblies in Wales and Northern Ireland. These were elected partially on the basis of **proportional representation** and were given certain powers over health, education, transport and enterprise, and in the case of the Scottish Parliament, some tax raising powers.

Voters in Britain have a wide range of mainstream parties to choose from:

- The **Labour Party** was founded in 1900 to represent working class interests. It threatened to take working class votes from the **Liberal Party**, who responded with a raft of reforms designed to appeal to the working class voter. However, from the 1920s the Labour Party supplanted the Liberals as the main opposition to the **Conservative Party**.
- In Scotland and Wales since 1945 there has been a growth of **Nationalist Parties**, with the Scottish National Party (SNP) given a considerable boost by the discovery of North Sea oil off the Scottish coast. These parties argued that they could represent the needs of voters better than parties with headquarters in London.
- Concerns with environmental issues and the reform of the Labour Party have also led to other small parties emerging, such as the **Green Party** and the **Scottish Socialist Party**. These have been given a considerable boost by the proportional system of election to the devolved Scottish Parliament since 1999, which has provided more representation for smaller parties.

Votes for women

The first movement set up by women to fight for votes, or suffrage for women, was the Suffragists (National Union of Women's Suffrage Societies – NUWSS). This was founded by Millicent Fawcett in 1887.

The Suffragists hoped to persuade MPs and other influential men that women had the right to take part in the political process. They did this by acting peacefully, campaigning through leaflets, discussion meetings and letter writing. In 1901–02, Eva Gore-Booth gathered 67,000 signatures from textile workers in northern England for a petition to parliament. This was effective in persuading around half of MPs to support the idea of votes for women by 1914.

Some women grew impatient with the Suffragists' methods, however. In 1903, Emmeline Pankhurst founded the Women's Social and Political Union (WSPU), nicknamed the Suffragettes. Together with her daughters, Christabel and Sylvia, she wanted to take more direct and militant action to win the vote – deeds, not words.

Suffragettes disrupted political meetings held by MPs, dug up golf courses, fire-bombed cricket pavilions, broke windows and chained themselves to railings. After 1909, when arrested, some Suffragettes went on hunger strike. The most famous incident involved a Suffragette called Emily Davison who died trying to stop the King's horse during the 1913 Epsom Derby horse race.

In Scotland, the Suffragettes were a part of the Federation of Scottish Suffrage Societies and their actions included burning down the medieval Whitekirk Church, Ayr Racecourse and Leuchars railway station.

World War One was a key turning point as the Suffragettes stopped their campaign in order to support the war. Women took over jobs in factories and on trams when men went to fight, showing that they had an important contribution to make to the war effort, particularly in munitions production.

Partly in response to the sacrifices of ordinary soldiers on the Western Front, the vote was extended to all men over 21 in 1918, including all working class men. It was argued by some that women with education and property (traditionally the measure of who should vote) should not therefore be excluded.

The Representation of the People Act of 1918 for the first time gave women over the 30 the right to vote and become MPs and gave the vote to the remaining 40% of men still excluded.

In 1928, women over 21 were given the right to vote on the same basis as men.

Top Tip

The Suffragettes made the most obvious impact on the struggle for votes for women. However, many would argue that the more peaceful methods of the Suffragists and the effect of the First World War played a greater role in winning votes for women. The views of sources that you come across may well reflect this difference of opinion.

Quick Test

1. Why was the Third Reform Act a breakthrough for representation in Britain?

2. What factors helped women to win the vote for the first time in 1918?

3. Why might the First World War be described as a turning point in the campaign for votes for women?

4. How did the development of new parties help to improve political representation in Britain?

Did you hit your target for this topic? Give yourself a mark out of ten.

Answers 1. For the first time the majority of voters were working class. 2. Campaigning by the Suffragists and the Suffragettes; women's role in wartime; the vote was given to all men for the first time while educated women remained without the vote. 3. It gave women a chance to clearly show their contribution to national life. 4. The Labour Party was created to represent working class people specifically, while nationalist parties in Scotland and Wales, gave people with nationalist ambitions someone to vote for.

Enquiry skills

Below are two sources and some questions that you might be asked in the Enquiry skills section of the exam paper.

You will first be given an issue:

New technology has brought success to British shipbuilding since the Second World War.

There will then be three questions for you to answer. The first will ask you how useful one of the sources would be to you in addressing the issue in the box. The second will ask you what evidence supports or argues against the issue. The third will ask you how far you agree with the issue.

Study the sources below carefully and answer the questions which follow. You should use your own knowledge where appropriate.

When tackling Enquiry skills questions in the examination, do not be afraid to write on the exam paper. Annotations, underlining and/or highlighting key words and phrases really help you to focus on the content of the source and the question that you have been asked.

Source A is from a recent book on industry in Britain by Watt and James.

> *Construction of British ships uses the latest technology. Welding has replaced riveting. Prefabrication means that building can be done in indoor sheds.*
> *New forms of propulsion mean that British ships are fit to sail anywhere.*
> *British shipbuilding can compete on price, quality and delivery.*

1. How useful is source A for investigating the state of shipbuilding since the Second World War?

3 marks

You might answer as follows:

Written by objective and expert authors, this source is very useful in giving specific and objective information about how the technology of shipbuilding has changed in the last 50 years. It suggests that by replacing riveting with welding and adopting methods such as prefabrication, ships can be built in British yards indoors in all weathers allowing British builders to compete with yards worldwide on price, quality and in meeting delivery deadlines. However, it fails to point out the problems in labour relations and demand that led to a declining share for Britain to just 2 per cent of world output by the mid 1980s.

- The candidate has put the answer into her or his own words rather than copying out large amounts.
- The candidate has clearly stated how useful the source is in relation to the question.
- The candidate has used some recalled knowledge to add to the answer, showing what has been left out.

Now tackle the other two questions below:

Source B describes the decline of Scottish shipbuilding.

> *The shipyards of the Clyde built some of the best ships in the world. Now, despite new techniques and improved materials, some shipyards are not able to go on working. New methods, such as welding instead of riveting, have failed to meet the threat from foreign competitors.*

2 What evidence is there in source A that technology has brought success to British shipbuilding? What evidence is there in source B that technology has not brought success to British shipbuilding? **4 marks**

3. How far do you agree that new technology has brought success to British shipbuilding since the Second World War? Use the evidence from the sources and your own knowledge to come to a conclusion. **5 marks**

You might answer as follows:

The authors of source A believe that the most up to date technology is used in the construction of ships in Britain. They give welding, prefabrications and new ways of propelling ships as examples of this. Their conclusion is that British shipbuilders are as competitive as any others around the world.

By contrast, the author of source B suggests that these new techniques, while improving production in British shipyards, have been insufficient to compete with competitors from abroad and so some have had to close down.

- Note here: it would be very tempting at this point to bring in additional information from recall about the other reasons, besides technological ones, why British shipyards were failing, (e.g. subsidies to Korean and Scandinavian shipyards; labour relations). However, the next question asks you for this and what has already been included above should be enough for 4 marks, so you would be better to save time and use this knowledge in the next question.

4. How far do you agree that new technology has brought success to British shipbuilding since the Second World War? Use the evidence from the sources and your own knowledge to come to a conclusion. **4 marks**

- State clearly whether you agree or disagree.

- First use information in the sources and then use the 'recalled' information that the sources have not included to support your answer.

- Write a balanced conclusion.

Top Tip

For 'how useful' questions it is often a good idea to have a routine to help you focus and develop your answer. For example, **Who** wrote this and why? **How** do they get their ideas across? Are there any key facts left out? To what extent is it useful?

Long term causes of war

Alliances

For war to have occurred on the scale of the First World War, two armed camps opposed to each other must have developed. This was greatly helped by the development of two **alliance** systems before 1914.

An alliance is an agreement between two sides to help each other if they are attacked.

Three major alliances were formed before the First World War:

- **Triple Alliance**: Germany, Austria-Hungary and Italy were allies from 1882.
- **Dual Entente**: France and Russia were allies from 1894.
- **Entente Cordiale**: Britain and France were allies from 1904. This was supposed to be a 'friendly agreement' rather than an actual alliance, but it became stronger in the following years, particularly as it was tested.

Testing the alliances

- **The Moroccan Crisis 1905-6**: The German leader, **Kaiser** Wilhelm II, wanted to test the new friendship between Britain and France and hopefully split them up. The French had agreed that Britain should control Egypt while France could take control of Morocco. The Kaiser publicly stated his support of the Sultan of Morocco's independence from France and demanded a conference in Algeciras. To the Kaiser's astonishment the French and British stuck together and he had to back down. The Entente Cordiale became stronger and the British and French started military talks.

- **Agadir Crisis 1911**: As the French took over Morocco, the Kaiser tried to intimidate the French into giving Germany some land. He sent the gunboat *Panther* to Agadir to make his point. The British Chancellor of the Exchequer, David Lloyd George, made a speech in London warning Germany not to threaten British interests, such as the Atlantic port of Agadir. The Kaiser was forced to back down again.

Imperialism

The **British Empire** controlled one quarter of the world in 1914. The French and Belgian Empires were also very large. The German Empire was only formed in 1870 and, although it had gained some land in the '**Scramble for Africa**', the Kaiser felt left behind. He wanted 'a place in the sun', i.e. an overseas empire like Britain. Britain and France saw this ambition as a threat.

British anxieties increased even further as its economic dominance in the world was also being threatened. Germany in particular was stealing its markets in steel, engineering and chemicals.

Militarism

Naval race: The development of the *Dreadnought* battleship by the British in 1906 threatened to make much of Britain's massive navy obsolete. The news that Germany was building its own battleship created panic in Britain. When Germany built four ships, the newspapers demanded, 'We want eight and we won't wait'.

Top Tip

Britain's imperial interests and island state made the navy especially important. By 1914 the British had almost twice as many Dreadnoughts as Germany, but had to patrol the whole of their extensive empire. The **'two power standard'** was a principle of British policy that insisted that the British Navy should at least match any two other powers combined.

Nationalism

- **Nationalism** is the idea that each country puts its own interests first. Before 1914, prestige and not losing face were guiding principles of foreign policy for Germany, Britain and most other countries.

- The idea of nationalism was also especially important in the Balkan countries. As the old Turkish (Ottoman) Empire began to fall apart, nationalities such as the Bulgarians, Greeks and Serbs fought for their independence, and for as much land for their new countries as possible. In 1912–13 there were two Balkan wars out of which Serbia emerged twice as big as it had been before.

- Austria and Russia both hoped to make gains from Turkey's weakness. In 1908 Austria-Hungary annexed Bosnia-Herzegovina. This was a blow to Russian prestige and to the ambitions of Serbia.

The Balkans in 1914

Quick Test

1. What were the two opposing power blocs in Europe in 1914?

2. How did the actions of the Kaiser serve to strengthen the Entente Cordiale?

3. Why did the naval race create increased tension between Britain and Germany?

4. Why were the Balkans important to both Russia and Austria-Hungary?

Did you hit your target for this topic? Give yourself a mark out of ten.

Answers 1. The Triple Alliance (Germany, Austria-Hungary, and Italy) and the Triple Entente (France, Russia and Great Britain). **2.** By threatening France in Morocco he pushed France and Britain closer together. **3.** Because the British considered having the biggest navy of vital importance, while the Kaiser wanted a navy to win an overseas empire like Britain's. **4.** As the Turkish Empire fell apart, Austria-Hungary felt threatened by Serbia, while Russia wanted a port in the Mediterranean and to defend other Slavic countries like Serbia.

Short term causes of war

The assassination of Archduke Franz Ferdinand

The heir to the Austrian throne, **Franz Ferdinand**, was shot dead on 28 June 1914 while visiting the capital of Bosnia, **Sarajevo**. He was shot by Serbian student Gavrilo Princip, who had links to the **Black Hand terrorist group**, which was in turn loosely connected to the Serbian Government. This provided an opportunity for Austria to cut back growing Serbian power.

Austria-Hungary and Serbia

- Austria-Hungary issued an **ultimatum** to Serbia, with a list of demands, including control of the Serbian police force.

- **The blank cheque:** Austria-Hungary got support from the Kaiser that they would have support whatever action they took against Serbia. This meant Austria-Hungary no longer had to worry about Russian support for Serbia.

- Austria-Hungary declared war on Serbia on 28 July 1914. Russia began to mobilise its huge army in support of Serbia. It did this because both Russians and Serbs were Slavs with strong cultural links in language and religion. Also, Russia could not lose face again as it had when Austria-Hungary had annexed Bosnia.

Top Tip

All of the 'trigger causes' mentioned here are linked to the long term causes mentioned on pages 44 and 45. Draw up a table to make these links. This should help your understanding of what happened.

The Schlieffen Plan

- **The Schlieffen Plan** was designed ten years before the outbreak of the First World War by General von Schlieffen. It was the German military plan to deal with the alliance of France and Russia without having to fight a war on both a western and eastern front.

- Efficient use of the railways was designed to move troops quickly to the west, through Belgium and Luxemburg to knock out France within weeks, then rapidly to the east before the enormous process of Russian mobilisation had been completed.

- Once the Russians began their mobilisation, it would be a race against time for the German generals if they were to take on both France and Russia.

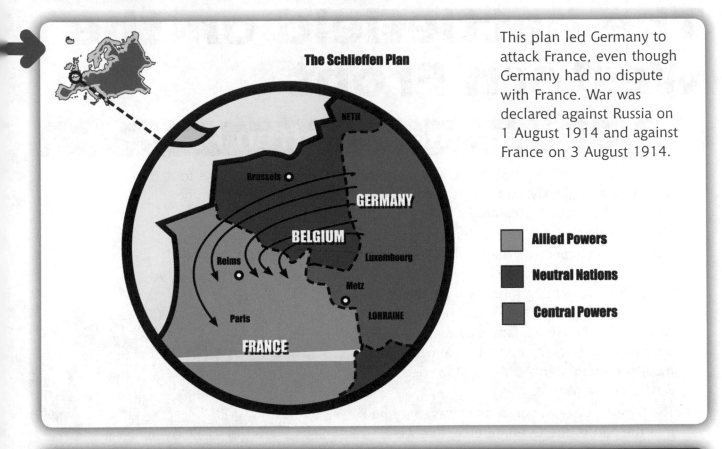

The Schlieffen Plan

This plan led Germany to attack France, even though Germany had no dispute with France. War was declared against Russia on 1 August 1914 and against France on 3 August 1914.

- Allied Powers
- Neutral Nations
- Central Powers

NETH
Brussels
GERMANY
BELGIUM
Reims
Luxembourg
Metz
Paris
LORRAINE
FRANCE

Britain and war

- Germany had hoped that Britain might stay out of the war.
- The Entente Cordiale had become stronger in the years leading up to 1914.
- Rivalry with Germany, particularly naval rivalry, made many British believe that a war with Germany was likely at some time.
- For many the invasion of Belgium was crucial. The neutrality of Belgium had been guaranteed by the **Treaty of London 1839** and it was a small country, being bullied by a large one. Government and public opinion supported war, declared on 4 August 1914.

Quick Test

1. Why did the Austrian Government blame the assassination of Archduke Franz Ferdinand on Serbia?

2. Why did the Russians feel that they had no choice but to mobilise in support of Serbia?

3. What was 'The blank cheque'?

4. How did the Schlieffen Plan help to turn the Balkan Crisis into a Europe-wide war?

Did you hit your target for this topic? Give yourself a mark out of ten.

Answers 1. On the surface because Franz Ferdinand was killed by a Serbian nationalist, but in reality Austria-Hunagary wanted an excuse to go to war with Serbia. **2.** Russia had been too weak to help Serbia when Austria Hungary had annexed Bosnia Herzegovina in 1908 and had felt humiliated. The Russians would not let that happen again. **3.** It was the Kaiser's promise to help Austria-Hungary whatever she did against Serbia. **4.** As soon as it was clear that Russia was supporting Serbia, the German generals wanted to launch a surprise invasion of France as soon as possible and before the Russians were ready, to avoid fighting both France and Russia at the same time (a 'war on two fronts'). It also meant going through Belgium. This, along with Britain's entente with France, brought Britain into the war too.

The battlefield on the Western Front

The failure of the Schlieffen Plan

Von Schlieffen's Plan was designed to use the speed of the German railways to knock out France quickly, so that the German Army could be redeployed in the east to face the Russian 'steamroller'. The plan failed.

- The Belgians, British and French put up much stiffer resistance than the Germans had expected. The Belgians fought fiercely and the 100 000 strong **British Expeditionary Force** (BEF) proved a much more effective fighting force than the Kaiser's taunt of 'that contemptible little army' had suggested. Meanwhile, the French famously commandeered taxis from Paris to ensure that there were enough men to stop the German Army at the decisive **Battle of the Marne**.

- The German General von Moltke was concerned that the part of the German forces that were attacking directly through France on the left of the swinging arm of the army was not strong enough. So he took troops from the right to reinforce them. This weakened the attack through Belgium, slowing it down and allowing the British and French to organise their defence.

- German supply lines became stretched and the troops became exhausted.

Top Tip
Legend has it that von Schlieffen's dying words were 'Let the right wing be strong'. Many people have therefore blamed von Moltke for the failure of the German attack. Thinking about whether or not you agree with this will help you to understand and remember the details of the start of the war.

Consequences for the war

The failure of the Schlieffen Plan had important consequences for the war:

- The Germans now had to face a war on two fronts; the Western and Eastern.

- Once the German Army was stopped, both sides tried to outflank each other in a period known as '**the race to the sea**'. Having reached the Channel, all along the front, both armies started to dig trenches. These soon stretched from the coast to the Swiss border.

- This **stalemate** allowed the British Navy to impose a blockade of Germany that would eventually strangle its ability to supply the German population and army.

Top Tip
The First World War was a war of defence. It was much more difficult to attack than to defend. As you read on try to think of three reasons why this should be.

New technology and the Western Front battlefield

The First World War was fought by armies backed by mass factory production. Factory machines could produce millions of shells, bullets and chemicals, and artillery, machine guns, gas shells, and later tanks and aeroplanes.

- **Heavy artillery**: the main method of attack was to fire tens of thousands of shells in a barrage against the enemy trenches before a mass infantry charge. The battlefield quickly became churned up and muddy, and filled with craters.

- **Machine guns**: these gave a decisive advantage to the defenders in battles on the Western Front. Two machine gunners would feed hundreds of rounds of ammunition on belts into a machine gun that sprayed them into oncoming infantry.

- **Gas** was used first by the Germans in 1915, then by the French and British. Chlorine, phosgene and mustard gas were the most deadly, but it was not a decisive weapon because the wind could blow the gas in the wrong direction, and the development of gas masks lessened its impact.

- **Tanks** were first used by the British at the **Battle of the Somme** in 1916. Although slow moving (maximum speed 4 mph) they were very frightening for the first Germans who saw them. However, they were liable to breakdown and were difficult to operate. It was only at the **Battle of Cambrai**, in 1917, that the British learned to use them in large groups to punch through enemy lines, at which point they became much more effective.

- **Aircraft** were initially used, along with balloons, for observation purposes, to make artillery more accurate and spot enemy movement. Later, however, mounted machine guns that could shoot through propellers without damaging them made aerial dogfights possible and a few were even able to drop small bombs.

Quick Test

1. Why did the Schlieffen Plan fail?
2. What were the consequences of its failure?
3. Why were machine guns particularly useful for defence?
4. What limited the effectiveness of gas and tanks on the Western Front?

Did you hit your target for this topic? Give yourself a mark out of ten.

Answers 1. Resistance was stronger than expected: the right wing of the attacking force was too weak; supply lines became stretched. **2.** German war on two fronts; stalemate; trenches. **3.** Two machine gunners could stop hundreds of attacking infantry soldiers. **4.** Gas was not accurate, depended on the wind and gas masks made it ineffective. Tanks could often break down.

A soldier's life on the Western Front

The trenches

The war on the Western Front was a war of **attrition** (it was about how many men and shells each side could employ, not about manoeuvres). Hundreds of thousands of men volunteered for the army in the first few weeks of the war, usually in **pals battalions** made up of friends or work colleagues. Many assumed that 'it would all be over by Christmas'. By 1916 there still were not enough soldiers to meet the huge demand for recruits, so **conscription** was introduced. All men between 18 and 40 were liable to be 'called up'. Soldiers spent two to three weeks at a time in front line trenches.

Life in the trenches was not pleasant. The following were common:

- Mud and water lined the trenches – this led to trench foot and gangrene.
- There were lice and rats.
- Soldiers were often blinded from gas attacks.
- To eat, there was only bully beef and dry biscuits.
- There was constant noise from shelling.
- There were lots of snipers, so periscopes were used to prevent soldiers having to look over the top of the trench.
- Many soldiers suffered from shell shock; a mental condition caused by the constant threat of death, noise and the sight of friends being maimed or killed close by.

no man's land

parapet   barbed wire

firestep

mud and water

British Trench

The daily routine

When young men joined the army in 1914–15, many did so in search of adventure and action. Fear that it would be over by Christmas and they would miss out was part of the reason why there was such a large response to the recruitment campaigns in the early months. However, the daily reality of fighting trench warfare, while certainly fraught with danger, often seemed far from the heroic dreams of cavalry charges and dramatic acts of courage:

- Most of the time there was no attack; boredom was a problem.
- Most work was done at night, leading to lack of sleep and exhaustion.
- There was a lot of digging and trench repair to be done, as well as repairing barbed wire.
- Patrols were needed to spy on enemy trenches.
- Many soldiers had to delouse others.
- They had to do a lot of weapon-cleaning.
- There was also tunnelling to be done to set explosive charges.
- The soldiers snatched sleep in shallow 'dug outs'.
- They had to 'stand to' at dawn in case of enemy attack.
- They could only 'stand down' at dusk.

Going over the top

For the British Empire troops and French in particular, whose job it was to try to move the Germans out of their entrenched positions in Belgium and France, it was necessary to climb out of the discomfort, but relative safety, of the trenches and advance across the muddied and cratered landscape of no man's land. Because the weapons of the First World War favoured defence, the tactics used led to particular suffering and hardship for the side carrying out an offensive:

- A preliminary bombardment was supposed to clear the way. However, it warned the enemy of attack and churned up the ground.
- When soldiers went over the top they often got caught in the barbed wire.
- They could easily be gunned down by machine guns.
- There were huge numbers of casualties, for example, 60 000 British soldiers were killed or wounded in one day of the Battle of the Somme.

Quick Test

1. What was no man's land?

2. Why did hundreds of thousands of men volunteer in the early months of the war?

3. Identify five problems that soldiers had to put up with on the Western Front.

4. What were the key features of a trench on the Western Front?

Did you hit your target for this topic? Give yourself a mark out of ten.

Answers 1 The land between the sets of trenches on either side. 2. Adventure; their friends were joining up; afraid to miss out in case it was 'all over by Christmas'; propaganda. 3. Mud and water – trench foot and gangrene; lice and rats; blinding from gas attacks; bully beef and dry hard biscuits; noise from shelling; snipers – (periscopes were used to prevent having to put your head over the top of the trench); shell shock (a mental condition induced by the constant threat of death, noise and sight of friends being maimed or killed close by). 4. Barbed wire; mud; parados and parapet; dug out; fire step; zig-zags.

The Home Front in Britain

Defence of the Realm Act

In the First World War, civilians were involved more than in previous wars. The **Home Front** was just as important as places where the fighting happened. The government became increasingly involved in people's lives.

From 8 August 1914 the Defence of the Realm Act (DORA) gave the government sweeping powers:

- Prices were controlled and hoarding declared illegal.
- Censorship was introduced.
- Spying was tackled as flying flags, bell ringing and spreading rumours were banned.
- British Summer Time created more daylight for work, and pub licensing tried to curb the effects of drunkenness at work.
- Trade unions were restricted. Farm work, coal mining and railways, and later munitions factories were **nationalised**.
- Foreign nationals were arrested and even deported.

Despite these controls, by 1917 meat, sugar, butter, margarine, bacon and ham had to be **rationed**. The introduction of the **convoy system** by David Lloyd George, Prime Minister from 1916, saved Britain from starvation as German U boats sank dozens of supply ships.

Top Tip
DORA makes it easier to remember the Defence of the Realm Act. If there are other key ideas that you have difficulty remembering, try making up your own names for them.

Recruitment

- A famous poster campaign, led by **Lord Kitchener** (Minister for War) encouraged people to sign up to war by using propaganda about German atrocities committed in Belgium. The expectation of 100 000 recruits was exceeded, with 0.5 million joining in August 1915 and 3 million by the end of 1915.
- Pals battalions encouraged friends and workmates to join up together, for example, the players and supporters of Hearts football club formed the 'MacRae's Battalion'.
- Women handed out white feathers (a symbol of cowardice) to young men not in uniform to put pressure on them.
- The thirst for travel and adventure was also a strong incentive to join the army.

"YOUR COUNTRY NEEDS YOU"

By 1916, the number of casualties and the length of the war meant that recruitment declined, so **conscription** was introduced for all men aged 18–41 (the **Military Service Act**).

Conscientious objectors had to face a tribunal. Some went into non-fighting roles, such as ambulance drivers or stretcher bears, others were imprisoned.

Top Tip

Try to connect the information here in a 'ripple diagram'. Imagine 'the declaration of war' is a pebble thrown into a pond. The first ripple might include government control, then DORA, then recruitment, etc.

How lives changed

The war affected almost everyone. People's relatives died, there were bombings, and there were food shortages. Recruiting created labour shortages, so the roles of women changed.

- Women went to work on the land in the **Women's Land Army**.
- '**Munitionettes**' worked in arms factories. The dangerous chemicals turned their skin yellow, so they became known as 'canaries'.
- Middle class women, such as Vera Brittain, who wrote about her experiences, became nurses or ran family businesses.
- Women could also join the forces, in the Women's Royal Naval Service (Wrens) or the Women's Army Auxiliary Corps (WAACs).
- The campaign for votes for women was suspended to help the war effort.

At the end of the war almost all women lost their jobs to men returning from the front. However, the award of the vote to women over 30 in 1918 is often seen as a reward for women's work in the First World War.

Quick Test

1. Why was the Home Front considered by many to be as important as the Western Front?

2. How did the government try to ensure sufficient supplies of food and military equipment?

3. Why did so many young men volunteer to join the British Army in 1914–15?

4. What new jobs were undertaken by women to support the work of the Home Front?

Did you hit your target for this topic? Give yourself a mark out of ten.

Answers 1. The Home Front had to supply the men and weapons to win the war of attrition. **2.** By rationing. **3.** Propaganda; peer pressure (did not want to be called a coward); their friends joined up in 'Pals' Battalions; thirst for travel. **4.** Worked in munitions factories; nurses; ran family businesses; country labouring (Women's Land Army).

The Home Front in Germany and the end of the war

The impact of the war on German civilians

As in Britain, hundreds of thousands of men joined the army, although in Germany there was conscription from the start. The government also rapidly took control over industry. Life was generally much worse for German civilians than it was for the British. The key fact of the war for German civilians was the **British Naval Blockade** that was imposed from the beginning of the war. Germany was dependent on imports for many of its basic needs and the armed forces were the first to be supplied. This left very little for the rest of the population.

- Parks and flowerbeds were converted for vegetable growing.
- Substitute foods were developed, such as chestnut flour.
- Meat production declined by 42 per cent, milk by 50 per cent, butter by 40 per cent.
- During the 'Turnip Winter' of 1916–17 potatoes ran out completely.
- There were severe shortages of rubber, metals and other materials vital for the war effort.
- Workers trying to survive on a fraction of the calories required each day were much less productive.
- By 1917 there was severe rationing, and by 1918 the threat of starvation.
- The Germans were more vulnerable to disease due to hunger and were particularly affected by the influenza epidemic that killed hundreds of thousands of people across Europe in 1918.

Top Tip

There are many reasons for German defeat in the First World War, but they cannot all be equally important. To help you think about the reasons for defeat, write out nine causes of defeat on a piece of paper, cut them out then arrange them into a diamond shape with the most important cause at the top, the two next most important underneath, etc.

The end of the war

Throughout the stalemate of the war on the Western Front, the Germans had the advantage of fighting a defensive war, as they were in occupation of French and Belgian territory. The British, the French and their allies had to drive them out. However, the Germans were fighting a war on two fronts. This was exhausting and costly in lives and in economic terms. By the time that the **Russian Revolution** (November 1917) and Russian surrender (March 1918) allowed the Germans to concentrate their forces on the Western Front, they faced the additional enemy of the USA and its huge resources of men and equipment, brought into the war by unrestricted submarine warfare by the Germans against allied shipping.

The **Spring Offensive 1918**, also called the Ludendorff Offensive, the Peace Offensive, Operation Michael or the Kaiserschlacht (Kaiser battle), was the last throw of the dice by the German Army. They broke through the enemy lines and morale soared. However, shortages of supplies slowed the offensive by June and the allies, bolstered by the contribution of US troops and supplies, counterattacked and rapidly reversed the German gains of the Spring. Morale in Germany plummeted and by September it was clear that Germany could not win. The allies demanded the removal of the Kaiser.

In late October 1918, the German Navy at Kiel and Wilhelmshaven mutinied and strikes and further mutinies in the army quickly spread. Germany soon began to look like revolutionary Russia.

Moderate German politicians hoped to prevent a revolution by demanding the removal of the Kaiser. The Social Democrats declared the abdication of the Kaiser and the creation of a new Republic, and on 10 November the Kaiser escaped from Germany to Holland.

An **armistice** (truce) ending the fighting was signed, ending the war on 11 November 1918.

Quick Test

1. Think of three reasons that led to the war being more difficult for the Germans than for the British.
2. How many German soldiers died in the First World War?
3. Why did the Spring Offensive fail?
4. When did the First World War end?

Did you hit your target for this topic? Give yourself a mark out of ten.

Answers 1 The British Naval Blockade; shortages of food; shortages of rubber, metals and other resources 2. 2 million 3 Shortages of German supplies; American soldiers rapidly joining British and French allies. 4. 11 November 1918

The Treaty of Versailles

Following the armistice of November 1918, the war was ended by the treaties signed during 1919–20. By far the most significant was the **Treaty of Versailles (June 1919)** that settled the position of Germany.

The Big Three

In June 1919 the world leaders met in the Palace of Versailles outside Paris to create the post-war world. Quickly it became clear that **The Big Three** would dominate. Each had their own priorities.

Woodrow Wilson, President of the United States, had written 14 points or ideas about how Europe should be organised to prevent war. These had been rejected by Germany as the basis of peace at the start of 1918. They included:

- **national self-determination** (each country to get its own democratic government)
- disarmament
- an end to 'secret diplomacy' (all negotiations should be through public treaty)
- the creation of a **League of Nations** to settle all future disputes.

Georges Clemenceau, Prime Minister of France, saw Germany as the source of all Europe's troubles. He demanded **reparation** for France's huge losses during the war, and the destruction of Germany's power.

David Lloyd-George, Prime Minister of Britain, had recently won an election by suggesting that he wanted to punish Germany. He was keen to get financial reparation to help rebuild the British economy. However, he was concerned that Germans would turn to **Communism** if the treaty was too harsh. He worked for compromise.

Terms of the treaty

Britain and France had been seriously affected by the war, and Germany had imposed harsh terms on Russia in the **Treaty of Brest-Litovsk**, so Wilson allowed the treaty to reflect French and British aims more than his.

- Alsace-Lorraine was returned to France.
- Eupen and Malmedy were given to Belgium.
- North Schleswig was given to Denmark.
- West Prussia and Posen were given to Poland creating the **Polish corridor**. Danzig became a '**free city**' under League of Nations control.
- The Saar was to be under League control for 15 years, then there would be a **plebiscite** (vote) to decide if it was French or German. France to use the coal mines within the Saar until then.
- Estonia, Latvia and Lithuania were to become independent states.

- Union (Anschluss) between Austria and Germany was banned.
- Germany lost all of her colonies.
- The German Army was limited to 100 000 men.
- No German submarines, battleships or military aircraft were permitted.
- Germany had to pay reparations, set at £6 600 000 in 1921.
- To justify the reparations, Clause 231 the '**War Guilt Clause**' blamed Germany alone for the war.
- A League of Nations was set up to settle future disputes.

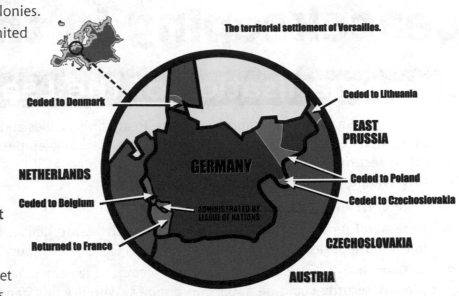

The territorial settlement of Versailles.

Ceded to Denmark
Ceded to Lithuania
EAST PRUSSIA
NETHERLANDS
GERMANY
Ceded to Poland
Ceded to Belgium
Ceded to Czechoslovakia
ADMINISTRATED BY LEAGUE OF NATIONS
Returned to France
CZECHOSLOVAKIA
AUSTRIA

Reactions to the treaty

The terms of the treaty satisfied virtually no-one:

- The German public were outraged. The treaty did not follow the idea of national self-determination as many Germans were left outside Germany, and the military seemed too small to defend Germany effectively. The financial clauses would impoverish Germany. Most distressing was the fact that the treaty was a '**diktat**', a dictated peace over which the Germans had no say. Germany alone could not be blamed for the war. The German people had removed the guilty Kaiser.
- The French were disappointed that Germany had not been weakened further.
- At first the treaty was welcomed in Britain, but the British gradually came to see the treaty as too harsh and unfair to Germany.
- The US Congress refused to **ratify** (to pass) the treaty because they feared the League of Nations would drag the USA into too many international disputes.

Quick Test

1. What was the armistice and who were the Big Three?
2. What kind of treaty did Woodrow Wilson want Versailles to be and why did Clemenceau demand a harsh treaty?
3. Why did the Germans object to the territorial terms of the treaty?
4. Why did the USA refuse to ratify the treaty?

Did you hit your target for this topic? Give yourself a mark out of ten.

Answers 1 A ceasefire (agreement to stop fighting). The Big Three were: The USA (Woodrow Wilson): France (Georges Clemenceau) and Great Britain (David Lloyd-George). **2.** Fair to all. Clemenceau demanded a harsh treaty because France had suffered the most and blamed the Germans. **3.** Many Germans would be left outside Germany and Germany was split in two – this went against Wilson's idea of national self-determination. **4** Congress did not want America to be dragged into international disputes.

The League of Nations and peacekeeping in the 1920s

The organisation of the League

The League of Nations was established by the Treaty of Versailles and came into operation on the same date, 10 January 1920. Its **covenant** aimed to keep the peace through **collective security** (if one country is attacked all should act as if they have been attacked themselves) and to tackle a variety of social problems.

There were five main bodies:

- The **General Assembly**: All 55 members met each year to deliberate on the general direction of policies. Crucially, all decisions had to be unanimous.
- The **Council**: This dealt with particular problems as they arose, recommending how collective security could be applied to disputes. With Britain, France, Italy and Japan making up its four permanent members, all decisions had to be unanimous.
- The **Court of International Justice**: This was based in the Hague. It applied international standards of law and justice, dealing with legal disputes between states.
- The **Secretariat**: This was the League's civil service.
- **Committees and Commissions**: These dealt with issues arising from treaties and social problems such as child labour, refugees, health and women's rights.

Problems that the League had to deal with in the 1920s

The League had very little influence over these disputes:
- War between Poland and Russia.
- War between Turkey and Greece.

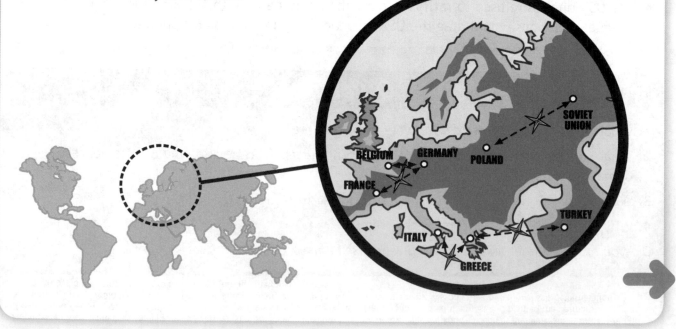

- **Corfu incident**, 1923: Italy bombed Corfu to try to extract compensation from Greece.
- In 1923, France and Belgium invaded the Ruhr region of Germany to secure reparations payments from Germany.

The League did have some successes:

- It acted quickly to end a Greek incursion into Bulgaria, ensuring that damages were paid by Greece.
- A dispute between Sweden and Finland over the Aaland Islands was rapidly settled in favour of Finland.
- The League used a plebiscite (vote) to divide Upper Silesia between Germany and Poland.
- Mosul was granted to the new British mandate of Iraq in a dispute with Turkey.

The work of the Refugee Organisation, the International Labour Organisation and the Health Organisation were also areas of success for the League. However no progress was made with disarmament and more powerful countries seemed inclined to ignore the League.

Top Tip

To organise the information in this section, draw a line down the middle of the page and write 'success' at the top of one column and 'failure' at the top of the other. Then list things you regard as successes and failures for the League.

Why did the League find it difficult to keep the peace?

- **The Treaty of Versailles**: The League was linked to it. The Germans saw the League as a 'winners club' and preferred to work outside it. The French saw the League as the means to enforce the Treaty of Versailles, but Britain didn't, so France acted alone.
- Membership: Some powers, most importantly the USA, were not members of the League. Germany was excluded until 1926 and Russia until 1934. These countries were never committed to it.
- Alternative solutions: Because of the Treaty of Versailles and because strong countries had to get unanimous support for action, alternatives were often found. The Ruhr crisis was resolved through the **Dawes Plan**. The **Locarno Agreement** of 1925, in which Germany recognised its western borders agreed at Versailles, by-passed the League, as did the **Kellogg-Briand Pact** (1929) which declared that war should not be an instrument of diplomacy. These alternatives helped to undermine the credibility of the League by ignoring it.

Quick Test

1. What is meant by collective security?
2. How did the League settle the dispute between Poland and Germany over Upper Silesia?
3. Give three examples of disputes that the League failed to settle.
4. Why was the absence of the USA such a serious blow to the League?

Did you hit your target for this topic? Give yourself a mark out of ten.

Answers 1 If one country is attacked all countries act as if they have themselves been attacked. **2.** With a plebiscite (a vote) **3.** War between Poland and Russia; war between Turkey and Greece; the Corfu incident. **4.** The USA was one of the most powerful countries in the world and the League was an American idea in the first place.

Enquiry skills

In **Source A** Sir Arthur Conan Doyle writes about a gas attack in 1915.

> *Poison gas was a dreadful weapon which most cruelly affected the victim. The Germans won ground using the methods of the mass murderer. Their great army became in a single day an object of tremendous horror and great contempt.*

1. Discuss the attitude of the author of Source A towards the use of poison gas.　　　4 marks

In your answer:

- Make sure that you clearly state whether the author is for or against the use of poison gas.
- Give reasons for your answer using specific points in the source.

In **Source B** a British soldier writes about the aftermath of a gas attack.

> *We have heaps of gassed soldiers. The poor things are burnt all over with great blisters and blind eyes all glued together. They speak in the merest whisper saying their throats are closing and they will choke.*

2. How fully do sources A and B describe the use of gas in the First World War? You must use your own knowledge and give reasons for your answer.　　　5 marks

In your answer:

- Get yourself into a routine for 'how fully' questions like this one.
- Consider the **provenance** (where the source comes from). Is this an eye-witness account (which of the authors had actually seen a gas attack take place)? How might this affect how full their account of a gas attack could possibly be?
- Extract at least one (perhaps more) things that each source says about gas attacks and at least one or two things that you know that both sources have left out.
- Conclude by saying clearly whether the sources give a complete picture or whether they only tell part of the story.

Top Tip

Each mark for this question will require you to write a developed point. Once you have stated a point that the author is making, you need to explain it, using your own knowledge to help you. If you do this well, two good points should be enough. If you are not sure and if you have the time you could make three or more points.

Source C gives extracts from the covenant of the League of Nations.

> *The aims of the League of Nations are to settle disputes among nations and prevent war.*
>
> *Members of the League of Nations recognise that keeping peace requires national armaments to be reduced.*
>
> *Any member country going to war against another member shall be said to have committed an act of war against all members of the League.*
>
> *All members shall immediately cut off all trade with any state which breaks the covenant.*

3. What are the views of the authors of the covenant about what the League of Nations should do?

5 marks

In **Source D** a modern historian describes some of the problems which faced the League of Nations.

> *As a peacekeeping body the League of Nations was a failure. An organisation which professed to be in favour of peace and prevent war still allowed its members to keep armaments. There was also a lack of will power to make it work. To take action against a member who broke the rules of the covenant required all member nations to act together and that rarely happened.*

4. How far do Sources C and D agree about the League of Nations?

4 marks

Top Tip

When comparing sources, it is important to remember to compare them directly and specifically, that is, you should try to make it clear that you are pointing out similarities and differences between the two sources. If you just write about one source and then about the other one, you will not necessarily be making the comparison that the question asks you to make. You could quote individual words or short phrases to show where the sources agree or disagree.

Hitler's foreign policy

Adolf Hitler became Chancellor of Germany in January 1933 in the midst of the crisis that followed the **Great Depression**. He quickly became the **dictator** of Germany and began to prepare the country for war and expansion.

Rearmament and Hitler's aims

Hitler wrote his ideas down in *Mein Kampf* (My Struggle) in 1925. He outlined the following aims for German foreign policy:

- To destroy and overthrow the hated Treaty of Versailles.
- To build up Germany's military strength through rearmament.
- To create 'living space' (**Lebensraum**) for Germans by expanding German borders in Europe.
- To create a Greater Germany including all Germanic peoples, such as those in Austria and Czechoslovakia.
- To assert the superiority of the German 'master race' over the Slavic peoples of eastern Europe.
- To destroy Communism.

These aims implied that Germany would recover the lands lost in Europe under the Treaty of Versailles, such as the 'Polish corridor' that divided Germany in two, and that there would be wars in the east with Poland and Russia at the very least. For this Hitler would need to build up his armed forces far beyond the limits set by the Treaty of Versailles. He took the following steps to rearm Germany in the 1930s:

- As soon as he came to power Hitler started rearming secretly.
- At the **Disarmament Conference** of 1933 he demanded equal disarmament by other powers to match Germany. Hitler walked out when this demand was not met.
- In the next two years German expenditure on arms increased threefold and doubled again in the following three years.
- In 1935 conscription was introduced, designed to build up the German army to half a million men.
- In 1935 the British Government recognised and tacitly approved German rearmament by signing the **Anglo-German Naval Treaty**, permitting a German Navy 35 per cent of the size of the British Navy, including military aircraft, battleships and submarines banned by the Treaty of Versailles. In 1936 the Luftwaffe was tested out for real in support of Franco in the **Spanish Civil War**. Famously the town of Guernica was destroyed by the 'Condor Legion'.

NEW ALLIES

Japan

Italy

VERSAILLES

MASTER RACE

COMMUNISM

LEBENSRAUM

Top Tip

Have a look back at the section on the Treaty of Versailles in Unit IIB. Note two things: firstly why Hitler's foreign policy would help to make him more popular, secondly note five ways in which Hitler's actions overturned the Treaty of Versailles.

Growing tension

The 1930s was a decade of increasing international tensions. This was not always a result of German actions. In 1931 the Japanese invaded Manchuria in Northern China. To balance the threat of Hitler in Europe, Britain and France tried to build closer links with Italian dictator Mussolini, signing the **Stresa Front** (1935). However, Mussolini decided to follow the example of Japan and invaded Abyssinia. Weak League of Nations sanctions and public condemnation of Italy's actions drove Italy closer to Germany. In 1936 the **Rome-Berlin Axis** (the 'Pact of Steel') was signed.

However, it was Hitler's actions that did most to increase the threat of war in Europe:

- In March 1936 German troops were moved into the Rhineland, which had been de-militarised by the Treaty of Versailles.

- In 1934 an attempt by Hitler to increase his influence in Austria had been blocked by Mussolini, then suspicious of German power. In March 1938, following a campaign of protest and disruption by the Nazis in Austria, Hitler invaded Austria to carry out the union (**Anschluss**) explicitly banned by the Treaty of Versailles. Although German-speaking, Austria had not been a part of Germany before the First World War.

Top Tip
Draw a flow diagram to get a picture of how actions by Japan, Italy, Britain and France seemed to affect how Hitler acted in rearmament and expansion. Leave some space to add more as you read through the next section on Appeasement.

Quick Test

1. What was 'Lebensraum'?

2. What Treaty did Britain sign with Germany in 1935?

3. Why did Hitler putting troops into the Rhineland (which was a part of Germany) cause tension?

4. What was the 'Pact of Steel' and what was the Anschluss?

Did you hit your target for this topic? Give yourself a mark out of ten.

Answers 1 Living space for the German people 2 The Anglo-German Naval Treaty 3. This was not allowed under the Treaty of Versailles and was the first overt act of Nazi Germany's remilitarisation. 4. The alliance of Germany and Italy and the union of Austria and Germany.

Appeasement

Definition

Appeasement is the name given to the foreign policy followed by Britain in the 1930s. It meant avoiding war by finding what demands of aggressive nations might reasonably be met. Allowing Japan to invade Manchuria and Hitler to occupy the Rhineland in 1936, are examples of passive appeasement. In 1937 Neville Chamberlain became the British Prime Minister and followed active appeasement.

Top Tip

Because we know that the 1930s ended in war, appeasement seems very difficult to understand. However, there were reasons for it that seemed reasonable to many at the time. You should try to understand these.

Reasons for the policy of appeasement

CREDIT

- **Hatred of war**: Aerial bombing of civilians in the Spanish Civil War made the British public concerned that the next war would be even worse than the First World War.
- **The Treaty of Versailles**: It now seemed too harsh on Germany and needed revision.
- **The Depression**: Unemployment and poverty were severe; large sums of money could not be spent on weapons.
- **The League of Nations**: Its weaknesses meant that there were no peaceful alternatives to appeasement.
- **The USA**: The USA would have nothing to do with Europe, and France was politically divided, so Britain had no strong allies.
- **The USSR**: The Conservative Government of Britain saw Communist Russia as at least as big a threat as Nazi Germany.

The Czech Crisis and the failure of appeasement

- The **Sudetenland** in western Czechoslovakia contained a majority of German speaking people. It also contained factories, mountains and all of the Czech defences against German attack. Czechoslovakia was allied to the French.
- Hitler encouraged local Nazis to campaign for the Sudetenland to be given to Germany.
- Chamberlain and the French Prime Minister, Daladier, tried to persuade the Czechs to make concessions. Chamberlain flew to Germany unsuccessfully to try to work out a deal. War seemed unavoidable.
- Then, at the end of September 1938, Mussolini, the Italian leader, proposed a four power conference, excluding Czechoslovakia and Russia. This took place in Munich.

- They decided that Czechoslovakia would hand the Sudetenland to Germany in exchange for a guarantee that no further demands would be made. The Czechs were forced to agree.
- Chamberlain was treated like a hero on his return although some, such as Winston Churchill, condemned the agreement as a betrayal.
- In March 1939, Hitler put pressure on the Czechs to invite German troops in to 'restore order' in the rest of Czechoslovakia, and the Nazis occupied non-German territory for the first time.
- Attitudes towards Hitler became much more hostile.

Poland and the start of the war

Hitler now turned to Poland, with whom Germany had a non-aggression pact. He demanded that they surrender the port of **Danzig**. Britain and France assured Poland of help. Poland was too far away for France and Britain to help effectively, so negotiations were opened for an alliance with Russia. However, Stalin signed the **Nazi-Soviet Non-Aggression Pact** in August 1939 which divided Poland between Russia and Germany. A full scale German invasion into Poland was launched on 1 September 1939. A British ultimatum to Germany was followed by a declaration of war on 3 September 1939.

Quick Test

1. What was appeasement?

2. Give two examples of appeasement from before the Czech Crisis.

3. Which Prime Minister gave appeasement a boost in 1937?

4. Why did Hitler demand that the Czechs hand over the Sudetenland?

Did you hit your target for this topic? Give yourself a mark out of ten.

Answers 1. The policy followed by Britain and France of trying to avoid war by giving dictators what they wanted if it seemed reasonable. **2.** Japan invading Manchuria; Hitler occupying the Rhineland. **3.** Neville Chamberlain **4.** It contained a majority of German speaking people.

The Home Front in Britain

Protecting civilians

The Second World War was known as 'the people's war'. As in the First World War, the need to mobilise all of the resources of the country meant that the war affected everyone.

On 7 September 1940 the Germans bombed London in retaliation for an RAF raid on Berlin. This was the beginning of the **blitz** (the Luftwaffe's bombing of British towns and cities such as London, Coventry, Glasgow and Portsmouth).

Protection from bombing included the following:

- **Shelters**: Air raids usually happened at night. A loud siren gave warning of their approach. Anderson shelters built of corrugated iron and earth were constructed in gardens. Although useless against a direct hit, they could protect against shrapnel and falling buildings. Those who had no garden could sleep in the cage-like Morrison shelters. Damp, cold and uncomfortable, many people stopped using these types of shelters after a while. In London tube stations were also popular shelters.

- **Blackout**: To make it more difficult for bombers, Air Raid Precautions (ARP) ensured that all lights were turned out and that heavy blackout curtains were put up. Without street lights and proper car headlamps, accidents increased. White painted kerb stones and white lines in the middle of the road were used to reduce road deaths.

- **Gas masks**: These were issued to protect people from gas attacks, and tape was put on windows to reduce flying glass.

- **Evacuation**: Thousands of children were evacuated from towns and cities to the countryside. For many this was an adventure, as travel to the country was rare. For others it was a frightening experience and there were commonly misunderstandings between 'host' families in the country and city children used to a different way of life. When bombing did not begin in September 1939 and for months afterwards, many returned to the towns.

Top Tip

Sometimes it can be helpful for you to link key points to visual triggers in order to remember them, e.g. a semicircle for a bomb shelter, a black square for blackout, a simple train for evacuation, etc. Make up your own.

Food and work

In the 1930s, Britain imported 55 million tons of food from overseas anually. As German U-boats sank British shipping, a policy of **rationing** and **propaganda** was introduced to reduce waste, to grow more food and ensure fairness. Sugar, butter, bacon and ham were rationed early in 1940, soon to be followed by other food types. Posters, newspapers and newsreels encouraged the public to '**Dig for Victory**', to feed scraps to pigs and rabbits that could be eaten, and to hand in pots, pans and iron railings to make Spitfires and bombers (even though this was impossible). People were encouraged to feel a part of the fight against Nazism.

With the cost of the war rising upwards from £10 million (almost £1/2 Billion in today's money) per day, people had to be made to feel positive about the sacrifices they had to make. Nevertheless, while real wages rose because of the shortages of workers, extra money was more likely to be spent on goods that could be obtained on the **Black Market** (ie illegally) than on government bonds or schemes such as "Wings for Victory" that were supposed to encourage citizens to put their surplus wealth into the war effort.

Conscription was introduced 5 months before the war and extended to all men between 18-45. One and a half million men had been called up by the end of 1939. By the end of 1940, however, pleas from employers had led to the exemption of 200 000 men. Conscription was not extended to men over 40 until 1941 and single men were called up before married men. By the end of 1941, young single women were also called up for National Service. Around 20 out of every 1000 conscripts were **conscientious objectors**, but most had their appeals turned down in tribunals, especially in London, where the Blitz was worst. Those in reserved occupations or too old could join the Local Defence Volunteers – later called the Home Guard or 'Dad's Army'- to prepare for the expected invasion. Women took over work normally done by men in factories and transport or joined the Women's Land Army. By 1943, three quarters of women in Britain were involved in war work.

Top Tip
War on the Home Front would be a good subject for a ripple diagram. War might be the stone, with circles of ripples moving outwards showing the different effects of war.

Quick Test

1. What was the blitz?

2. What was a blackout?

3. Why do you think people were encouraged to hand in pots and pans and railings if these couldn't really be used to build military equipment?

4. How many women were involved in war work and what did they do?

Did you hit your target for this topic? Give yourself a mark out of ten.

Answers 1. The heavy bombing of British cities by the Luftwaffe. **2.** The extinguishing of all lights. It was against the law to keep lights on in case it made it easier for German bombers to hit their targets. **3.** It made people feel that they were a part of the war effort. **4.** 3/4 of women were involved in war work, such as working the land, operating transport or working in factories.

The Home Front in Germany

CREDIT

Propaganda and public opinion

- Early victories for the German Army in 1939–41 created high morale amongst Germans.
- Setbacks and increasing hardships created more discontent.
- Propaganda encouraged civilians to make sacrifices for the war effort. The vast majority fell into line.
- The Nazi police state discouraged any public show of discontent. Any sign of opposition was ruthlessly suppressed.
- Opposition did appear, e.g. **Edelweiss Pirates** were young people who tried to avoid conscription and listened to banned music such as jazz. There were attempts to assassinate Hitler from within the army, e.g. the **Stauffenberg plot**.

Top Tip
It is much more difficult to be sure how people in Germany felt about the war compared to what we know about people in Britain. Think about why this might be.

Shortages

- Food became increasingly hard to come by and rationing was introduced. The daily ration for a German civilian consisted of 12.5 oz of bread, 0.25 oz jam, 1.25 oz butter, fat, lard or bacon, 1.25 oz meat (although this was often not available at all) and 0.25 oz coffee (but this was often fake coffee).
- The Germans tried to make artificial copies of rare commodities such as rubber or oil, called 'ersatz'.
- There was a thriving black market in rationed goods.
- Because of Nazi racial policies, those who were not considered 'proper' Germans were seen as a drain on these scarce resources and received much less. Under the '**Final Solution**' the Nazis set about eliminating groups such as Jews, gypsies and the handicapped.

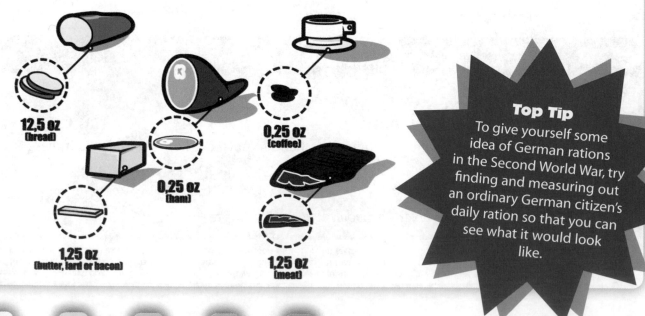

12,5 oz (bread)

0,25 oz (ham)

0,25 oz (coffee)

1,25 oz (butter, lard or bacon)

1,25 oz (meat)

Top Tip
To give yourself some idea of German rations in the Second World War, try finding and measuring out an ordinary German citizen's daily ration so that you can see what it would look like.

Devastation

- It was a matter of pride for the Nazis that German civilians would not be bombed, just as they had not been directly affected by the First World War or the **Franco-German War** of 1871. In the early years of the war this was largely the case and very few bombs fell on German cities.

- From 1943 the RAF and US air force bombed German cities to help the Russians attacking from the east. This culminated in the **thousand bomber raids**, in which bombing carried on day and night. Cities such as Dresden and Stuttgart were destroyed in firestorms created by thousands of incendiary bombs.

- Around 750 000 German civilians died. This compares with around 60 000 British civilians killed in the blitz.

- This bombing was supposed to destroy morale and military communications centres, but only around 25 per cent of the bombs fell within eight miles of their target.

Quick Test

1. Why was morale high in the early years of the war?
2. How did a few Germans show their discontent?
3. How many German civilians were killed by bombing during the Second World War?
4. How accurate was allied bombing of German cities?

Did you hit your target for this topic? Give yourself a mark out of ten.

Answers 1. The German army was doing well. **2.** They listened to banned music and some officers tried to assassinate Hitler. **3.** 750 000 **4.** Not very – 75% fell outside 8 miles of the target.

Weapons and tactics

Key weapons

Like many wars, it was the side with the greatest military resources that won the war. In this case the combination of Russia, the USA and the British Empire. The USA alone could produce over 70 000 tanks and 120 000 aircraft per year.

Defence fighter aircraft such as the **British Spitfire** and the German **ME 109** were faster and more manoeuvrable than anything previously. Even more important was the development of **strategic and tactical bombers**. Dropping incendiary devices and high explosives on civilian, military and industrial targets, large strategic bombers killed around 60 000 civilians in Britain and around 750 000 in Germany.

Often criticised as immoral and inefficient, heavy bombing of German cities probably played a decisive role in the defeat of Germany, diverting resources from fighting against the advancing Russians in 1944–45. Tactical bombers damaged and destroyed shipping, troops and supply lines. **RADAR** was developed by the British to provide early warning of air attacks and to find submarines.

Germany developed long range **rockets** called **V1** and **V2** that could reach London. By the end of the war the USA had developed the first **atomic weapons** and dropped two on Hiroshima and Nagasaki, killing over 130 000 civilians.

At sea, **aircraft carriers** were vital, allowing the use of a large number of aircraft in the open sea or over enemy territory without the need for a land base within range. German **U boats** made life very difficult for the allied war effort, sinking over 20 million tons of shipping.

On land the development of **tanks** and **troop carriers** since 1918 put a much greater emphasis on rapid movement. Heavily armoured and with a top speed of 20 mph, tanks could rapidly punch through enemy defences, allowing the encirclement of enemy troops.

Top Tip
To highlight how new weapons led to new tactics in the Second World War draw up a table with two columns headed weapons and tactics in the First World War and the Second World War.

Blitzkrieg

Blitzkrieg means 'lightning war'. Although developed by the British at the end of the First World War and experimented with by the Russians in the early 1930s, it was Germany's success in 1939–41 with blitzkrieg that showed its true value. It maximised the use of new technology.

- The key elements were speed and surprise.
- Motorised units of tanks and troop trucks moved rapidly through weak points in enemy defences.

- Communications and Command Headquarters were destroyed by bombers, artillery and parachuted infantry (paratroops).
- Bombing of towns and the use of **stuka** dive bombers caused roads behind enemy lines to be filled with panic-stricken refugees.
- Strong points in the enemy lines were cut off and encircled by advancing troops.

Destroy Communications and Comand Headquarters

Roads filled of refugees

Strong points cut

Moving Rapidly

Speed & Surprise

Allied forces used the ideas of rapid movement of combined types of forces to great effect in **Operation Overlord** (the invasion of Europe after D Day) and in the war in the Pacific (by 'island-hopping', US forces avoided Japanese strong points).

Top Tip
Find out about the tactics used in the war from sources such as library books, textbooks and school history sites on the Internet such as Spartacus and BBC History.

Quick Test

1. Why was the USA particularly important to allied victory in the Second World War?
2. What were the most useful defensive weapons of the war?
3. What difference did the development of tanks and motorised vehicles make to the tactics used in the Second World War?
4. What were the keys to the success of blitzkrieg?

Did you hit your target for this topic? Give yourself a mark out of ten.

Answers 1. They could call on vast resources. **2.** Fighter aircraft and radar. **3.** Rapid movement became very important. **4.** Speed and surprise

The decline of Britain

Before the Second World War, Britain was seen as one of the great powers in the world. After 1945, two Superpowers, the USA and the USSR emerged as much stronger than every other country.

The impact of war

The Second World War drained the British economy. Bombing had destroyed tens of thousands of houses, and factories that had not been damaged had been converted to war work. As well as the process of rebuilding, the new Labour Government elected in 1945 began creating a **National Health Service** and a **Welfare State**, all of which would be expensive. Wartime rationing was continued for several years after the end of the war.

In 1947 the USA introduced the **Marshall Plan**, which gave $13 billion to rebuild Europe, with Britain being the biggest beneficiary. This helped Britain, but it showed that Britain was not the power it once was.

Decolonisation

At the start of the Second World War, several European countries, including Britain had **empires** that stretched around the world. The British Empire was the biggest, covering huge areas in Africa, Asia, Australasia, the Caribbean, North and South America. Some colonies, such as Canada and Australia, had been **self-governing dominions** for a long time. By the mid-1970s almost all of these colonies had become **independent**.

- Nationalist movements had been growing for some time, e.g. the Indian National Congress.
- During the Second World War the Japanese showed that Britain and the other European countries could be beaten, while the idea that the war was about democracy led to demands for independence.
- The USA, the USSR and the United Nations were opposed to **imperialism** (having an empire).
- The British were the first to realise that they no longer had the economic or military strength to govern a large empire.
- India, Pakistan and Ceylon (now Sri Lanka) were the first to win independence in 1947.
- Beginning with the Gold Coast (now Ghana) in 1957, African and Caribbean colonies quickly followed.
- Many joined a new organisation called the **Commonwealth**.

Top Tip
The Second World War was a turning point in the decline of British power. Use a mind map to make clear all of the implications of the war for Britain at home and abroad.

Suez

The moment when the world realised that Britain was no longer a great power came in October 1956.

- Britain and France considered the **Suez Canal** which linked the Mediterranean to the Red Sea through Egypt as crucial to their trade and vital to their interests.
- The Egyptian leader, **Colonel Nasser**, wanted to assert Egypt's independence from European powers. He also opposed the establishment of Israel as a new state in 1948.
- He received help from Communist Russia and eastern Europe.
- He took control the Suez Canal, mainly owned by the French and British.
- The British Prime Minister, Anthony Eden, thought Nasser was a new Hitler and so, along with France and Israel, launched an invasion of the canal area.
- Afraid that this unpopular attack would drive Arab countries sympathetic to Egypt into Communist influence, the USA unexpectedly agreed with the USSR that this invasion was an example of French and British imperialism. Britain and France were forced to back down. Britain was humiliated.

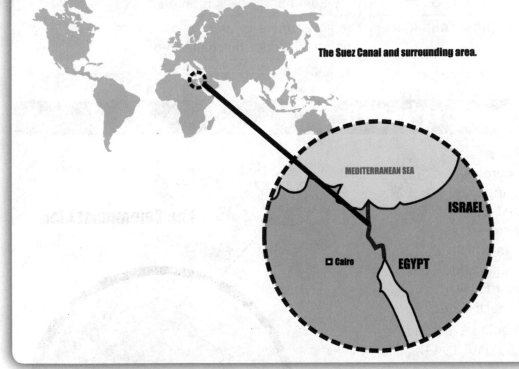

The Suez Canal and surrounding area.

Quick Test

1. Why was Britain economically less able to police a large empire after 1945?
2. How did the Second World War increase demands for independence around the world?
3. Which were the first countries to become independent after the Second World War?
4. How did Suez make it clear that Britain was no longer a great power?

Did you hit your target for this topic? Give yourself a mark out of ten.

Answers 1. Industry had been destroyed, the war had cost too much and the government's resources were stretched to breaking. **2.** Empires were made to look weak and people in the empires were encouraged to fight for democracy and freedom. **3.** India, Pakistan and Sri Lanka **4** Without American support the British had to back down.

The rise of the superpowers

Top Tip

To help you think more deeply about these important concepts, think of three reasons why Capitalism and Communism could not 'co-exist' easily.

Capitalism and Communism

The **Cold War** 1945–89 was about the ideological differences between US Democratic **Capitalism** and Soviet **Communism**. The key differences were:

US Democratic Capitalism	Soviet Communism
Private ownership of most businesses	The State owns most businesses
Individual ambitions are more important than preventing inequality	Wealth should be shared equally
Multi-party democracy	Only one party; the Communist Party
Free speech, debate, publication of ideas	Only Communist ideas promoted
Governments chosen or thrown out in free elections	The government created by a workers' revolution cannot be challenged

Stalin's foreign policy

During the Second World War the USA and the USSR were allies against Nazi Germany. However, Stalin suspected US intentions. Mutual suspicion turned into a Cold War, in which they refused to co-operate, issued propaganda and prepared for war, without directly fighting each other.

The Communist bloc.

- The allies delayed opening a 'second front' against Germany until 1944. Stalin believed that the USA hoped that Germany and the USSR would destroy each other.

- The USSR had suffered the greatest losses against Germany. Russia had been invaded by Germany twice as well as by many other countries in the previous 100 years. Stalin wanted to make sure that the USSR could not be easily attacked again.

- In conferences at Yalta and Potsdam in 1945, relations became cooler between East and West. President Truman kept the new US super weapon from Stalin. When atomic bombs were dropped on Hiroshima and Nagasaki by the USA, Stalin suspected that they were intended to be a warning to the USSR. The USSR had no nuclear weapons until 1949.

At the end of the war, Soviet armies were quick to establish Communist governments sympathetic to the USSR. Through Soviet influence, opposition politicians were harassed, elections rigged and the media manipulated until there were Communist governments in Poland, Hungary, Bulgaria, Albania and Rumania. This created a 'buffer zone' against invasion. Yugoslavia became Communist but refused to follow Stalin or the USSR.

US foreign policy

Before the war the USA had stayed out of problems in Europe. As troops came home, it looked like this might happen again. However, the US Government quickly decided that it had to remain involved in world affairs.

- Harry Truman was very anti-Communist, especially after meeting Stalin at Potsdam.
- In March 1946, Winston Churchill gave a speech at Fulton, Missouri in which he pointed out the danger of growing Soviet Communist power in eastern Europe. An '**iron curtain**' had fallen across Europe from 'Stettin in the Baltic to Trieste in the Adriatic'. Broadcast on radio, this speech influenced US public opinion.
- In 1947 the British had problems preventing Communism appearing in Greece and Turkey. In a statement, known as the '**Truman Doctrine**', the US President promised that the USA would help anyone fighting against the spread of Communism anywhere.
- The Truman Doctrine was backed up by the Marshall Plan (named after the US Secretary of State) which gave $13 billion to help Europe recover from war. It was regarded with suspicion by Stalin and no eastern European countries could accept it.

NATO and the Warsaw Pact

Twelve countries set up the **North Atlantic Treaty Organisation (NATO)** during the **Berlin Blockade** crisis in 1949, promising to defend each other should their freedom come under attack. The idea was to tie the USA into the defence of western Europe long term. When West Germany was permitted to join in 1955, the USSR set up its own organisation to co-ordinate their military forces, called the **Warsaw Pact**.

Quick Test

1. What was the Cold War?
2. Why did Stalin want to establish Communist governments in eastern Europe?
3. Why did the atomic bombs worry Stalin?
4. What was the Truman Doctrine?

Did you hit your target for this topic? Give yourself a mark out of ten.

Answers 1. A war of propaganda, spying and preparing for war without directly fighting each other, between the USA and the USSR. **2.** As a 'buffer zone' against future invasion **3.** He thought that they were intended as a warning against the Soviet Union. **4.** The American President's promise to help anyone fighting Communism anywhere.

The United Nations

Organisation

Set up in October 1945 under a charter drawn up in San Francisco, the **United Nations** (UN) was designed to replace the deeply flawed League of Nations. Like the League its aim was to preserve peace and avoid wars, while tackling social and economic problems and upholding human rights.

Initially there were 50 member countries, but by the mid 1990s there were almost 200 members. Its key organs were the General Assembly, the Security Council, the Secretariat, the International Court of Justice and the Economic and Social Council.

- The **General Assembly** was the forum for all member countries to meet. Although each had a vote, unlike the League, decisions did not have to be agreed by everybody. Its main function was discussion, supervision and election of non-permanent Security Council members.

- The **Security Council** was the key decision-making organ of the UN. It met frequently and dealt with each issue as it arose, taking action itself or inviting the Assembly to do so. Five members were permanent: the USA, USSR, Britain, France and China. A further six were elected for terms of two years. For any decision to be reached all five permanent members had to approve along with at least four other members of the Council. The permanent members therefore had a veto.

- Based in New York, the Secretary General of the UN led a large number of administrators in the **Secretariat**, who ensured that the daily work of the organisation ran smoothly.

- Fifteen Judges met in the Hague as part of the **International Court of Justice** to sit in judgement over disputes between states.

- Taking up by far the largest part of the UN's expenditure, the **Economic and Social Council** not only carried out work of its own in health, education, population, drugs and so on, it also co-ordinated the work of agencies such as the World Health Organisation, the United Nations Children's Fund (UNICEF) and the United Nations Educational, Scientific and Cultural Organisation (UNESCO).

Top Tip
Try drawing a diagram to illustrate the structure of the United Nations.

How successful has the UN been?

The UN has had its problems. The veto given to all permanent Security Council members meant that action was very difficult in areas affecting the biggest crises of the Cold War, since either the USSR or USA could stop action being taken that they did not like. For example, the invasion of Hungary and Czechoslovakia by the USSR in 1956 and 1968 were condemned by most of the UN, but nothing could be done.

The UN was more successful than the League, not just through the work of the Economic and Social Council, but also in peacekeeping. For example, in 1956 the UN played an important part in settling the Suez Crisis as, although vetoed by France and Britain, a resolution demanding immediate withdrawal of troops was passed by the Assembly 64 to 5, and France and Britain felt forced to accept this. 5000 UN troops were sent in to keep the peace as they withdrew.

Top Tip
Although this section has been written in the past tense, the UN is still going strong. Try to find out about its work today and compare its effectiveness with 1940–70.

ECON. AND SOCIAL COUNCIL

INTERN. COURT OF JUSTICE

SUEZ

HUNGARY 1956

CZECH 1968

COLD WAR

UN SUCCESS   **UN PROBLEMS**

Quick Test

1. Who were the five permanent members of the United Nations?

2. What were the key organs of the United Nations?

3. Why was the Security Council the most important organ of the UN?

4. Why was peacekeeping particularly difficult for the UN during the Cold War?

Did you hit your target for this topic? Give yourself a mark out of ten.

Answers 1. USA, USSR, Britain, France and China. **2.** The General Assembly, Security Council and Secretariat **3.** It made the most important decisions. **4.** Either the USSR, China or Russia would veto actions that their opponents wanted to take and vice-versa.

Problems in Berlin

The division of Berlin

According to the **Yalta Treaty**, at the end of the Second World War, Germany was divided into four parts, governed by the USA, Britain, France and the USSR. Berlin, which was in the middle of the Soviet sector, was in turn divided into four. The USA, France and Britain each controlled areas of West Berlin. When they pulled out, they united the three sectors into one, under a democratically elected government. The eastern part of Berlin remained a Communist state under Soviet control.

Berlin divided.

The Berlin Blockade

While the USA poured money into West Berlin under the Marshall Plan and took steps to replace Nazi Government with democratic government, the USSR took wealth out of East Berlin as reparations needed to rebuild the horrific damage done to the USSR by the German Army.

- It quickly became obvious to Berliners that they would be much better off under the democratic Capitalist system of West Berlin and so many began to move into the western sector.

- The introduction of a new currency in West Berlin made this all too obvious as it immediately became worth much more than the East German currency. West Berlin became an island of prosperous western Capitalism in the middle of Communist East Germany. This began to embarrass Stalin.

- Stalin was eager to test out how serious the USA was about the Truman Doctrine, so in June 1948, he ordered all routes by rail and road through East Germany to West Berlin to be shut down in a **blockade**.

- Determined to show that they meant business, US, British and French aircraft kept West Berlin supplied through an airlift that involved dozens of flights each day, feeding over 2 million civilians for almost a year.
- In May 1949, Stalin was forced to admit failure and re-opened connections to Berlin.

Top Tip
The airlift was the climax of the first phase of the Cold War. Think of five reasons why Berlin was so important in 1948.

The Berlin Wall

In 1961 a new Soviet leader, Nikita Khrushchev, again felt confident enough to try to challenge the West over Berlin. He felt that the new US President, John Kennedy was weak as Khrushchev had scored a propaganda victory over the USA the previous year by shooting down an American U2 spy plane and publicly displaying its pilot, Gary Powers.

By August 1961, 3000 refugees per day were pouring from impoverished East Berlin into West Berlin. Khrushchev tried to bully Kennedy into withdrawing from West Berlin. When this failed, he ordered the building of a wall to cut Berlin in two, with barbed wire and guard towers to prevent anyone escaping to the West. There were many attempts made to escape across the wall, some of which were ingenious and successful, others ended in escapees being shot. It was symbolically significant as it made real Churchill's warning about an iron curtain falling across Europe.

Top Tip
The Cold War is a very good topic for comparisons between two points of view. Make sure that you can see each event from both sides.

Quick Test

1. Why were West Berliners better off than East Berliners by 1948?

2. How did Stalin attempt to test out the Truman Doctrine?

3. How did US, British and French forces defeat the Berlin blockade?

4. Why did Khrushchev decide to build a 28 mile long wall across Berlin in 1961?

Did you hit your target for this topic? Give yourself a mark out of ten.

Answers 1. The Marshall Plan poured money in to the west while Stalin took wealth out of the East. **2.** He tried to cut off West Berlin. **3.** With an airlift **4.** To stop the huge number of refugees leaving East Berlin and embarrassing the Soviets.

The Cuban missile crisis

Causes of the crisis

- 90 miles off the coast of Florida, Cuba was important to the USA as a centre for US business and tourist interests. In January 1959 the Cuban dictator, **Batista**, was overthrown by revolutionaries led by **Fidel Castro**. Castro nationalised US oil refineries, factories and sugar plantations.

- In January 1961, the USA cut off diplomatic relations and imposed **sanctions** on Cuba. The USSR sent aid. In April, Kennedy approved a CIA (US Central Intelligence Agency) plan for Cuban exiles to invade Cuba with US support at the **Bay of Pigs**. The plan went terribly wrong and Kennedy took the decision not to launch a full scale invasion in support. He was humiliated and Castro declared himself to be a Communist.

- There had been a large build up of nuclear arms in the late 1950s; hydrogen bombs, intercontinental ballistic missiles and the first satellite, Sputnik (launched by the USSR in 1958). These all increased tensions and concern about nuclear weapons. In fact a missile gap had opened up between the USSR and the USA, with the USSR lagging behind.

- Khrushchev wanted to protect Cuba from further invasion threats and to balance the medium range missiles that the USA had placed in Turkey which threatened the USSR. At the request of Castro, he took the decision to place nuclear missiles in Cuba. In doing this, Khrushchev was also probably trying to test out Kennedy.

Top Tip

Tensions in the Cold War increased and decreased at different times. To put the Cuban missile crisis in context draw a graph showing how tensions increased or declined at different times.

Course and consequences of the crisis

- On 16 October 1962 US aerial photographs revealed the existence of missile bases on Cuba.

- Most US cities were in range of a 'first strike' attack.

- Kennedy was under pressure from generals to launch an invasion of Cuba.

- On 22 October, the photographs were made public and a blockade imposed on Cuba to prevent 25 Soviet ships landing missiles on Cuba. Kennedy could not be sure if there were already missiles on Cuba (in fact there were).

- Kennedy made it clear that any attack from Cuba would mean a full-scale attack by the USA on the USSR, and demanded that sites and missiles should be dismantled and removed.

- With the whole world expecting imminent war, the two leaders looked for a way out by telephone and letter.

- Meanwhile the USA boarded a Soviet ship looking for missiles and the Cubans shot down a U2 plane. Neither side took action.

- A public agreement was reached on 28 October. The missiles were to be dismantled in exchange for a promise from the USA not to invade Cuba. Secretly Kennedy also agreed to remove medium range Jupiter missiles from Turkey.

- In the wake of the crisis attempts were made to avoid another crisis by setting up a telephone '**hot line**' between Washington and Moscow to avoid war happening by accident.

- A **Nuclear Test Ban Treaty** was signed in 1963 between countries owning nuclear weapons.

- Khrushchev was removed as leader of the USSR a year later.

Top Tip

To help judge the outcome of the crisis, try writing out two lists of what outcomes would have ideally suited each of the two sides. Write 'The USA' at the top of one list and 'The USSR' at the top of the other. Compare the lists with the actual outcome.

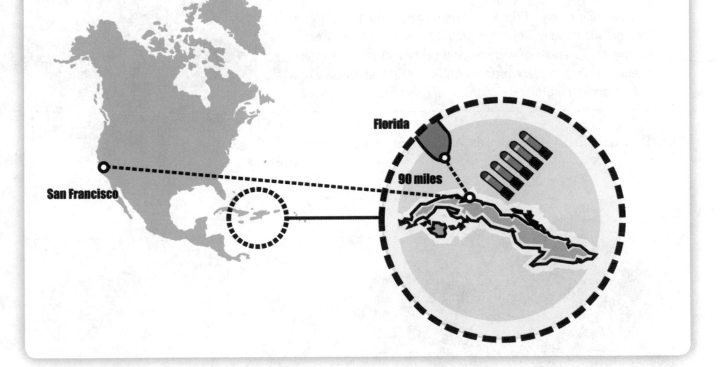

San Francisco

Florida

90 miles

Quick Test

1. Why did the Cuban revolution cause the USA concern?

2. Why did Cuba become allied to the USSR?

3. Why did Khrushchev decide to install missile bases in Cuba and how did Kennedy respond to the discovery of these missile bases?

4. What instances during the Cuban missile crisis might have led to nuclear war?

Did you hit your target for this topic? Give yourself a mark out of ten.

Answers: 1. It threatened US business interests and Castro's new regime could cause a strategic threat. **2.** The USSR offered aid when the USA imposed sanctions on Cuba. **3.** Khrushchev wanted to protect Cuba, threaten the USA and force the USA to withdraw missiles from Turkey. Kennedy demanded that all sites and missiles should be dismantled and removed. **4.** The USA boarded a Russian ship and the Cubans shot down an American aeroplane.

Enquiry skills

Study the sources carefully and answer the questions which follow. You should use your own knowledge where appropriate.

Source A is from a speech by Stalin about Soviet membership of the United Nations.

Even as members we do not trust the United Nations as a peacekeeping body. As a matter of fact the UN is not a united, worldwide organisation formed to keep peace. It is an organisation for the Americans acting for the needs of American aggression.

1. What was Stalin's opinion of the United Nations?   4 marks

Source B is by a modern historian.

The increasing rivalry of the Soviet Union and the United States made many question how 'united' the United Nations could be or how effective as a peacekeeping body. Any permanent member could use its power of veto to block proposals. This meant that America or Russia would prevent important decisions from being made.

2. To what extent do **Sources A** and **B** agree about the United Nations?   4 marks

Top Tip
Because the Cold War was a propaganda war there are lots of sources giving highly biased views for or against one side of the other. Source A is biased, giving only the Soviet point of view.

Top Tip
In answering this question note that one of the sources is primary and the other is secondary. Point this out in your answer and explain how this has led them to only partially agree. Be precise in quoting the points in the two sources where they agree and disagree. Come to a well-balanced conclusion to complete your answer.

CREDIT

In **Source C** Nancy Richmond remembers a German air raid over London during the Second World War.

> *The minute the siren went, all the Air Raid Precautions you had read were forgotten and fear took over the mad dash to the Anderson; the anxious fitting of gas masks and the waiting for the hated drone of the German bombers. I tried to appear calm, mainly for the children's sake. However, inside, I was churning. I had heard of other streets completely 'blitzed out'. Would we be next?*

3. Discuss the attitudes of the author in Source C towards an air raid.   5 marks

Source D is part of a broadcast by US President Kennedy on 22 October 1962.

> *These new missiles on Cuba include medium range ballistic missiles which are capable of striking Washington DC or any other city in the south eastern part of the United States. Other sites not yet finished are designed for intermediate-range ballistic missiles capable of striking most of the major cities in the western hemisphere.*

4. How fully does Source D explain the US view of the Cuban missile crisis? You must use your own knowledge and give reasons for your answer.   5 marks

Top Tip
When answering this type of question it is useful to sum up the author's overall attitude. Here her attitude is perhaps best expressed by the word 'fear'. But note that it is significant that the author was present during the air raid and speaks from first hand experience. Pick up on specific points in the source to develop and explain the reasons why the author is afraid.

Top Tip
With this kind of question it can be useful to think of ways to visualise your answer clearly. You might draw a circle or a square on your rough paper; put the points that the author (in this case, Kennedy) makes inside the circle and write any recalled points that are relevant outside the circle or square. This should help you to organise your answer clearly and make sure that you haven't left out anything important.

The Tsar's Russia 1: nation and government

Tsar Nicholas Romanov was born in 1868. In 1913 his family had ruled Russia for 300 years.

Prison house of the peoples

This is what the old Russian Empire was often called. The Russian Empire in 1900 was 100 times larger than Britain and very diverse in its population. In European Russia alone there were 16 different nationalities. There were over 100 million people, of whom just 55 million were Russian.

Russians were Orthodox Christians, spoke Russian and dominated politics, wealth and culture. The Tsar approved a policy called **Russification** in which all the different national and ethnic groups in the Empire were forced to follow Russian language and religious practices. Nearly one sixth of the Empire's people were Muslim. Each of the 25 nationalities in the empire had its own language, culture and, often, religion. Jews were subjected to a series of 'pogroms' designed to exclude Jews from society.

> **Top Tip**
> Although you will find a lot of faults with how the Russian Empire was ruled before and after the Revolution, remember that its size and its diversity made it a very difficult country to rule well.

The Tsar

An **autocracy** is a type of government where all of the power rests with one person. In Russia this person was the Tsar. This meant that the personality of whoever happened to be the Tsar was very important.

- Tsar Nicholas was a good and loving father but he was not a confident leader.
- His father had dismissed his ability to run the country. He was uncomfortable and indecisive in government.
- He was encouraged to hold on to and build up his autocratic powers by his German wife, Alexandra. He sometimes felt that he had to show he was strong and in charge when he would have been better to be cautious.
- Unknown to the country his only son and heir, Alexis, suffered from a disease called haemophilia, which meant that his life was always in danger and this constantly worried Tsar Nicholas.

Tsar Nicholas II

The Russian Government

- The Russian Government consisted of tens of thousands of officials who ran the affairs of the Russian Empire for the Tsar each day. There was much corruption and bribery and using your relations were the best ways to get what you wanted.

- The **Ochrana** (secret police) ensured that anyone who was a threat to the regime, or those who attempted publishing new ideas in books or newspapers, were arrested. Opponents of the regime were often sent into exile in Siberia.

- The Russian Army was not well trained or equipped, but it was very capable of suppressing opposition to the Tsar within the Empire. The officers were drawn from the nobility, ordinary soldiers from the peasantry.

- The Orthodox Church was extremely wealthy and powerful. The Tsar was the head of the church in Russia.

Up until 1905 there was no freedom of the press, and political parties only existed in secret. The massacre of peaceful demonstrators on '**Bloody Sunday**' in January 1905 led to the autocracy losing control as there was widespread support for strikes, demonstrations and riots. In a desperate attempt to win the support of the middle class, Nicholas issued the '**October Manifesto**' promising a **Duma** (Parliament), political parties and freedom of speech.

The Duma disappointed many 'liberals'. Nicholas remained 'the supreme autocrat'. The first Duma, elected mainly by the peasants, was more radical than expected and Nicholas regretted making concessions. The peasants were ruthlessly suppressed by new '**Land Captains**', electoral laws were changed to rig them in the Tsar's favour and the powers of the Duma were drastically cut back. New parties were harassed by the ochrana.

Quick Test

1. What made the Tsar powerful in Russia?

2. Why was Nicholas in many respects unsuited to be a tsar?

3. Why was Russia difficult to govern?

4. What was the Ochrana and what was the Duma?

Did you hit your target for this topic? Give yourself a mark out of ten.

Answers 1. He was the 'Supreme Autocrat'. **2.** He was indecisive and lacked confidence in his own ability. **3.** It was very large with a hugely diverse population **4.** The Ochrana was the secret service that suppressed any opposition to the Tsar; the Duma was the parliament that the Tsar set up in 1905.

The Tsar's Russia 2: Russian society

The Russian noble

- Although making up less than 2 per cent of society, nobles owned a quarter of the land in the Empire.
- They strongly supported the Tsar.

The Russian peasant

- 80 per cent of the population were peasants.
- They ate simple food such as cabbage soup, fish, rye bread or porridge.
- If the harvest failed, they starved; 400 000 died in the famine of 1891.
- The peasants had been **serfs** until 1861.
- Serfs had to repay large loans to the government in return for their inferior land.
- The majority lived in village communities, called **mirs**, in which all had to agree about how the land should be farmed
- Tensions were created in the countryside as, with the rising population, land became scarcer and the peasants' living conditions became increasingly difficult. This suffering was reflected in widespread peasant unrest between 1906 and 1908.

The Russian middle class

- A very small middle class had developed in towns and cities.
- Industrialists, lawyers, doctors and teachers were educated and developed their own ideas about how Russia should be run.

The Russian working class

- In the late nineteenth century, the Tsars encouraged more industry so Russia could compete with the industrialised powers such as America Britain and Germany.
- The biggest achievement was building the 6000-mile long Trans-Siberian railway which allowed the Empire to be crossed in a week.
- A 'working class' of ex-peasants made up 15 per cent of Russia's population by 1900.
- They had a poor diet and lived in poor, overcrowded housing.
- They worked long hours for low pay and accidents were common.
- All this created an unstable and dangerous atmosphere that the Tsar's government feared might lead to violence and revolution. The ochrana used spies and agents to prevent such dangers developing.

Top Tip
For the exam the key thing to note is how each of the groups contributed to the revolution of February 1917.

On the brink of war

Economic reforms

- Nicholas's second prime minister, Peter Stolypin, encouraged ambitious peasant farmers to do well. He hoped they would form a kind of rural middle class and would stop opposing the autocracy. Stolypin was assassinated in 1911.
- Meanwhile in industry there was tremendous growth in coal mining, oil and iron production, with businessmen and entrepreneurs becoming very rich.

Old problems got worse

- **Strikes**: Workers' wages did not go up, even as growth and profits did. Between 1912 and 1914 there were an increasing number of strikes, most notably in the Lena goldfields, where the strike was brutally suppressed by troops.
- **Opposition**: The new political parties included some who opposed the Tsar. The **Kadets** were liberals who wanted a constitutional monarchy like Britain. The **Social Revolutionaries** were the party of the peasants, including some former terrorists; they wanted a revolution to put power into the hands of the peasantry. The **Mensheviks** were Marxists who wanted to work towards a revolution of the working classes by supporting the Kadets. The **Bolsheviks** were waiting for an opportunity to carry out a rapid and violent revolution that would allow a workers' revolution led by the Bolsheviks.

Quick Test

1. Which was the largest social group in Russia?

2. Which social group most worried the authorities?

3. Why were workers particularly unhappy just before the First World War broke out in 1914?

4. What opposition groups challenged the authority of the Tsar in 1914?

Did you hit your target for this topic? Give yourself a mark out of ten.

Answers 1. Peasants **2.** The working class **3.** Workers' strikes were suppressed and peasants' land was becoming scarce **4.** Kadets; Social Revolutionaries; Mensheviks and Bolsheviks

The First World War and the fall of the Tsar

The problems that the Tsar's government had before 1914 may not have led to the **February Revolution**, but the outbreak of war was a crisis that the Romanovs could not survive.

The impact of the war in Russia

- At first there was a wave of support for the Tsar.
- The Russian army had huge numbers of soldiers, but they were poorly equipped. They suffered enormous losses in battles against the German Army.
- Nicholas's typically misguided sense of duty led him to take over direct control of the army in 1915, and he sacked several generals. This was a disaster; he became someone for the generals to blame for the losses, and it left the day to day government of Russia in the hands of his volatile wife, Alexandra.
- The Tsarina was German and she encouraged the Tsar to change ministers regularly. This led to rumours of a plot by the Tsarina and the monk Rasputin to undermine the Russian war effort. The Tsar's apparent inability to see the problem undermined his authority. In late 1916 Rasputin was assassinated by Prince Yusupov.
- The war and the army's demands meant that inflation and food shortages became an increasing feature of the war. The strike movement re-emerged in 1915. This was made even worse in late 1916 with a particularly harsh winter.
- From 1915 the Liberals, businessmen and local politicians complained that the autocratic Tsar was not allowing them to help win the war, with the resulting incompetence and corruption of government leading Russia to military defeat. They demanded a government of national confidence and meanwhile organised supplies for the war effort. The Tsar ignored them.

Top Tip
The assassination of Rasputin was a symptom of the attitudes that had developed towards the Royal Family, not a cause of the February Revolution. His assassination made no difference.

February 1917

- Tension was building in Petrograd due to the hard winter, strikes, lock outs, low wages and inflation.
- On International Women's Day (23 February/8 March) there were queues for bread and news that rationing of bread was to be introduced. Many women demonstrated and called on men to join them; the Putilov engineering workers joined them. By the weekend a general strike had begun.

- On 27 February/12 March troops were ordered by Nicholas to fire on crowds. The troops were mainly new recruits from the country waiting to go to the front. They switched sides and turned on the police, opening prisons. 1500 people were killed over the next few days. The **Petrograd Soviet** and the **Provisional Committee of the Duma** were set up to try to control events. The Petrograd Soviet issued Order Number One which said that soldiers did not have to obey their officers.

- Politicians and generals now believed that Nicholas was not respected enough to restore control. On 2 March/16 March the Tsar **abdicated** (give up the throne) for himself and his son in favour of Grand Duke Michael. The Grand Duke refused the throne and so the Russian monarchy came to an end. This was a big surprise to everyone. The illness of the Tsar's son was not widely known and most people had thought that he would take over.

Top Tip

After the revolution Russia adopted the same calendar as the rest of the western world. Up to that point the Russians used a calendar that was two weeks behind the rest of Europe.

Top Tip

In 1914 the Russian capital changed its name from St Petersburg to Petrograd to make it sound less German. In 1924 its name was changed again to Leningrad.

Quick Test

1. Why was Nicholas's decision to take over control of the army a mistake? (Try to find three reasons.)

2. Who started the February Revolution and why?

3. What finally made the Tsar abdicate?

4. Why was it a surprise that the monarchy ended so quickly?

Did you hit your target for this topic? Give yourself a mark out of ten.

Answers 1. He couldn't blame anyone else for problems; it left the Tsarina in charge; it lost him the support of the generals **2.** Women demonstrating about bread rationing and shortages. **3.** The mutiny of the army and the advice of his generals **4.** No one thought that Nicholas would abdicate for his son as well as himself.

The Provisional Government

Power problems

The abdication of Nicholas II was only the beginning of the Russian Revolution. Between February and October 1917 (March to November in the western calendar) the Provisional Committee of the Duma tried to act as a provisional government until the time was right to organise elections to a Constituent Assembly that could decide on a new government for Russia. However, the problems that it faced were great and before elections took place the revolutionary Bolshevik Party overthrew the **Provisional Government** and established itself as the new government of Russia.

Who was in the Provisional Government?

At first the Provisional Government was composed of middle class and noble Liberal members of the Duma. It was led by Prince Lvov. The Minister for Justice was the only socialist, **Alexander Kerensky**. He was the only member who was also in the Petrograd Soviet that was established on the same day (27 February). He carried messages between these two important bodies.

When, in April 1917, it was discovered that the Foreign Minister Paul Miliukov, who was in favour of the war, had been lying about the extent of the government's commitment to war, he resigned along with several other ministers. Kerensky became Minister for War and there was a coalition of Liberals and Socialists from the Petrograd Soviet.

The Provisional Government's problems

The new government faced very serious difficulties from the beginning:

- **Credibility**: The Provisional Government was not elected. Its members, some of whom had been in the Duma, simply declared themselves to be the government. The majority were well to do Liberals who believed in free speech and democratically elected governments. However, if they called an election they would lose to the Mensheviks or Social Revolutionaries who wanted to end the war and take wealth and land away from richer Russians.

- **Dual power**: A more democratic body was the Petrograd Soviet that met in the same building (the **Tauride Palace**) that the Provisional Government met in. The members of the Soviet were delegates who had been sent by groups of workers, soldiers and peasants to represent them. Made up mainly of socialists, the Petrograd Soviet believed that its job was to keep an eye on the Provisional Government and repeatedly interfered, but would not itself be the government. This situation was called 'dual power'.

- **The war**: The Petrograd Soviet controlled the army through '**Order Number One**' which said that the soldiers' first loyalty was to the Soviet and not to the Provisional Government. Members of the Soviet wanted to end the war as soon as possible, whether Russia's allies Britain and France liked it or not. Members of the Provisional Government appeared to agree with this, but secretly they wanted to fight on alongside Britain and France until the war was won. When this became public in April 1917 there was a scandal and socialists, led by Alexander Kerensky, took over the Provisional Government. But the increasingly unpopular war still went on and thousands of soldiers began to desert.

The Provisional Government was faced by problems in the war, economy and credibility.

The Petrograd Soviet was made up with workers, soldiers and peasants.

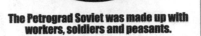

Dual Power in the Tauride Palace.

- **The economy**: One of the reasons that the war was so unpopular was because it was ruining the Russian economy. Inflation and food shortages got worse and worse. Also, the peasants demanded that more of the land that they worked should be given to them, but **land reform** was always put off, even after a pro-peasant Socialist Revolutionary joined the government. The peasants began to take land for themselves.

Top Tip

During 1917 all parties other than the Bolsheviks joined the Provisional Government. Therefore they were all blamed for its weaknesses. Only the Bolsheviks escaped blame.

Quick Test

1. What is meant by 'Dual Power'?

2. What was unique about Kerensky as a part of the revolution?

3. Why did the Provisional Government find it difficult to persuade people to do what it wanted?

4. How was the Provisional Government's policy towards the war different from the Petrograd Soviet's policy?

Did you hit your target for this topic? Give yourself a mark out of ten.

Answers 1. The Provisional Government was in charge in theory, but the Petrograd Soviet had more power. **2.** He was the only person in both the government and the Petrograd Soviet from the beginning. **3.** It hadn't been elected and people listened more to the Soviets which had been elected. **4.** The Provisional Government wanted to fight on until the war was won alongside Britain and France; the Petrograd Soviet wanted to end the war as soon as possible without giving up too much.

The Bolsheviks take over

Several factors put the Bolsheviks in the best position to take advantage of the Provisional Government's problems. This led to the **October Revolution** of 1917.

The April Theses

When **Lenin**, the Bolshevik leader, was smuggled into Russia by the Germans in April 1917, he transformed the position of the Bolshevik Party by issuing a declaration of intent, called **The April Theses**:

- The Bolsheviks were now the only party that would have nothing to do with the Provisional Government.
- The Bolshevik slogan 'All Power to the Soviets' campaigned for the more popular Soviets to run the government instead.
- Other slogans tapped into the concerns of Russians in towns, cities and (to an extent) the countryside, e.g. 'Peace, Bread and Land'.
- Their opposition to the war made the Bolsheviks especially popular with soldiers and sailors.

The Kornilov Coup

Lenin did not get everything right.

- In July 1917 he supported riots and demonstrations calling for the overthrow of the Provisional Government. Kerensky ordered the Bolshevik **Red Guard** to be rounded up and thrown in prison. Lenin had to escape in disguise to Finland.
- However, the Bolsheviks were lucky. In August General Kornilov marched on Petrograd, threatening Kerensky if he did not take stronger action against the Bolshevik 'spies'. Kerensky felt forced to release and arm the Red Guard, while Bolshevik agitators infiltrated Kerensky's army. Kerensky clearly needed Bolshevik support to maintain his government even though, as a more moderate socialist, he opposed them.
- The Bolsheviks were suddenly heroes and Lenin had been proven right about the Provisional Government. Bolshevik support in the Soviets soared.

Top Tip
Think about whether the Provisional Government's weaknesses or the Bolsheviks' strengths were more important in leading to the success of the October Revolution.

Leadership

The Bolsheviks had several able leaders, but Lenin and **Trotsky** stood out in 1917.

- Lenin persuaded his reluctant colleagues that the time was right to make a grab for power again in October.
- Trotsky had only joined the party in 1917. However, he was already well known from the 1905 revolution and quickly became chairman of the Petrograd Soviet.
- Trotsky organised the Bolshevik takeover through the Soviet's **Military Revolutionary Committee**.

The takeover

- Trotsky set up the Bolshevik HQ at the Smolny Institute the day before the takeover.
- Overnight the Red Guards and Bolshevik soldiers seized key points, such as bridges, post offices and railway stations.
- On 25 October the streets were quiet, there was little public support for either the Bolsheviks or the Provisional Government.
- Kerensky escaped the city to raise support.
- The cruise ship Aurora sailed up the River Neva and fired blank shells.
- On 26 October the Bolsheviks attacked the remaining Government Ministers in the Winter Palace and captured them at 2 a.m.
- Trotsky declared victory of the **Workers' Revolution** to the **All Russian Congress of Soviets**. Most non-Bolshevik delegates walked out. Trotsky said that they were walking into '**The Dustbin of History**'.

Quick Test

1. How did the April Theses help the Bolsheviks win popular support? (Think of three reasons.)
2. Why was General Kornilov's attempted takeover a turning point in 1917?
3. Why were Lenin and Trotsky important to the Bolsheviks in 1917?
4. Why did the Bolsheviks announce the victory of the takeover in the Congress of Soviets?

Did you hit your target for this topic? Give yourself a mark out of ten.

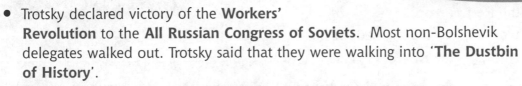

Answers 1. They promised to end the war; they promised all power to the Soviets; they promised bread. **2.** It made Kerensky look weak and made the Bolsheviks the saviours of the revolution. **3.** Lenin was the determined leader that inspired the Party to take over power. Trotsky was well known in the Soviets and he organised the October Revolution. **4.** So that it would seem that they had taken over power for the Soviets and the people and not just for themselves.

Civil war

Bolshevik Government

The Bolsheviks were not in control of the whole of Russia in 1917. There was a civil war going on.

They tried to deliver the promise of Peace, Bread and Land:

- They issued decrees on land and peace. Peasants would be allowed land and there should be a peace with Germany 'without annexations'. Workers were given control of the factories.

- The Germans continued to drive back the Russian Army. Trotsky was eventually forced to accept a humiliating peace at **Brest-Litovsk** in March 1918, losing one third of European Russia, including 74 per cent of its iron and coal production, and paying 300 million roubles of reparations.

- Lenin was confident that they would get everything back when the revolution spread and peace with Germany would allow them to fight new enemies inside Russia.

They dissolved the Constituent Assembly

- Elections to the **Constituent Assembly** had been called for November 1917. The Bolsheviks hoped that their popular decrees of October 1917 would help them to win.

- In the event they won the elections in the towns and cities, but the peasants overwhelmingly voted for the **Socialist Revolutionaries**, so the Bolsheviks shut the Assembly down after one day. The Socialist Revolutionaries went east to Samara and set up an alternative government.

They carried out a Red Terror

- Following the assassination of the German ambassador and opposition within the Bolshevik Party, Lenin set up the **Cheka**. Members of this secret police arrested and executed opposition. This was called the **Red Terror**.

- As the civil war worsened so did the Red Terror.

Top Tip

In 1919 the Bolsheviks changed their name to the Communist Party. You may see either term used in examination questions.

The course of the war 1918–21

There were three main stages to the war.

1. Fighting the Komuch and Czech Legion

- The **Komuch** were the remains of the Constituent Assembly. In 1918, they had the support of 40 000 Czech prisoners of war who had fallen out with the Bolsheviks. They defeated the Bolshevik Red Army very quickly and forced them to organise a better army.

- The Czechs wanted to get back home and claim independence. The new **Red Army** helped them do this, so the threat ended.

2. 'White' Generals surround the 'Reds'

- There were three main White armies fighting against the Red Army under the leadership of three generals: Yudenich in the North, Deniken in the South and Kolchak in the East.

- In the Autumn of 1919 the three armies put pressure on the Reds. The Bolsheviks moved the capital to Moscow.

- Throughout the war the White armies had problems co-ordinating their attacks.

3. Fighting the Poles

- By the end of 1920 the new threat was the Poles who tried to extend their new country's borders by taking land from Russia. A huge effort by the Red Army pushed them back and took the fight into Poland itself, before the Red Army was stopped and pushed back.

Top Tip

It is possible either to see the Reds as very clever to have outwitted the Whites in the civil war, or you could argue that the Reds had all the advantages from the start and were always very likely to win. Look out for these different viewpoints in sources.

Why the Reds won

The Reds won the civil war for four main reasons.

1. **Control of the heartland**: In 1918, the Reds got back much of what had been lost at Brest-Litovsk.

2. **Good leadership**: Lenin and Trotsky were outstanding leaders, ruthless in using terror and creating the 3 million-strong Red Army.

3. **White divisions**: The White generals refused to work with moderate socialists and did not co-ordinate their attacks. The Whites hanged peasants who had taken land for themselves.

4. **Control of the revolution**: Only the Reds could use the railways for transport, communication and propaganda.

Quick Test

1. Why did dissolving the Constituent Assembly and signing the Treaty of Brest-Litovsk both make a civil war very likely in Russia?

2. What advantages did the Reds possess over the Whites in the Civil War?

3. Why was Trotsky important in helping the Reds to win the civil war?

4. Why did the Whites fail to win popular support?

Did you hit your target for this topic? Give yourself a mark out of ten.

Answers 1. These actions created a lot of bitter enemies opposed to the Bolsheviks. **2.** They occupied the centres of population and industry and controlled internal lines of communication through the railways. **3.** He organised and inspired the Red Army. **4.** They represented the landlords and the return of the Tsar.

War Communism and the New Economic Policy

During the civil war the Bolsheviks were desperate to take any measures that might help them to win, so they adopted a very harsh policy called **War Communism**. By the end of the war it was clear that this policy could not last, so Lenin replaced it with something called the **New Economic Policy** in 1921.

War Communism

- Private trade was banned and factories were taken over by the government.
- Old factory managers were returned to work as production in worker-run factories was falling.
- Military discipline in factories was enforced by the Cheka.
- Rationing prioritised soldiers and munitions workers.
- Peasants were forced to hand over their grain to requisition squads.
- Money became worthless and barter (exchanging goods) was used instead.

Some on the left of the Communist Party welcomed this new policy as they thought it led to a fairer distribution of wealth and resources. However, it also caused incredible suffering:

- The taking of grain (requisitioning) was combined with Red Terror in the countryside. Peasants protested by refusing to grow more than they needed for themselves.
- There was severe rationing of food in the towns.
- In 1921 around 5 million people died in a famine in the richest grain-producing areas of Russia.
- There was a severe shortage of wood and fuel.
- Workers' conditions got harder and many left the cities.

The Kronstadt Mutiny

By March 1921 the civil war was all but won, but then something happened that made Lenin realise how serious the situation had become.

- The sailors of the Kronstadt Naval base had always been the most loyal supporters of the Bolsheviks.
- In March they mutinied, demanding a return to the freedoms for workers promised in October 1917; free elections, toleration of other parties and freedom for peasants to grow and sell their own crops.
- Trotsky was ordered to crush the mutiny, which he did.

- Lenin realised that, while he would not allow more freedom of speech, he would have to change his economic policy to save the Communist Government.

- FREE ELECTIONS

- TOLERATION

- PEASANTS TO OWN THEIR CROPS

The New Economic Policy

Under the New Economic Policy (NEP):

- Peasants were allowed to sell surplus grain once a basic tax had been paid to the government.
- 'NEP men' organised and profited from this trade.
- Factories employing less than 20 workers were allowed to operate independently.
- Markets in towns opened again.
- A new currency was introduced and foreign investment encouraged.
- The government continued to control large factories, heavy industry, railways, electricity and the banks.

The NEP succeeded in restoring grain and livestock production to pre-war levels by 1925 and created a consumer market, helping light industry. It was only partially successful in restoring iron and coal production.

Top Tip
Although the Communists liberalised the economy, they tightened their political control. There was no toleration of opposition.

Quick Test

1. Why did many Communists like War Communism?

2. Why did War Communism cause extensive suffering in Russia?

3. What made Lenin realise that he had to change policy?

4. How successful was the New Economic Policy?

Did you hit your target for this topic? Give yourself a mark out of ten.

Answers 1. It meant the end of capitalism and money. **2.** So much food was taken by force there was starvation. It was enforced by Red Terror. **3.** The mutiny of the Kronstadt sailors. **4.** It helped feed people again, but would not industrialise Russia quickly.

Stalin takes over

CREDIT

Who was Stalin?

- His real name was Joseph Dzhugashvili.
- He came from Georgia, a non-Russian province of the Russian Empire.
- After a time training to be a priest, he read Karl Marx, the author of the *Communist Manifesto* and left to join Lenin, whom he much admired.
- He first distinguished himself as a bank robber, helping to furnish funds for the Communist Party.
- Although on the Central Committee of the Party from 1912, he was undistinguished until he played a role in the civil war leading the defence of the city of Tsaritsyn (later renamed Stalingrad, now Volgograd).
- His big break came when he was appointed General Secretary of the Communist Party in 1919.

Top Tip
Many Russian revolutionaries used secret code names to avoid being arrested by the ochrana. Lenin was born Vladimir Ilych Ulianov, while Lev Bronstein called himself Trotsky after one of his prison guards. Dzhugashvili originally called himself 'Koba the bear', before settling on 'Man of Steel' (Stalin).

The struggle for power

- Lenin suffered a series of strokes from 1922 and he was very ill throughout 1923, before dying in January 1924.
- There were several candidates to take over from Lenin as leader, but the most prominent were Stalin, the General Secretary of the Party, and Trotsky, who had organised the October Revolution and who took much of the credit for victory in the civil war.
- Stalin was not a great speechmaker and he came up with very few new ideas. His colleagues called him 'the Grey Blur' and 'Comrade card-index'.
- Stalin was regarded as a hard worker and he held several posts in the government and in the Communist Party in addition to being General Secretary, such as Commissar for Nationalities and Head of the Inspectorate of the Peasantry. He was able to use his positions to build up support for himself within the party. As the party became more important during the civil war, new members were encouraged to look to Stalin for leadership.
- Trotsky was much more 'glamorous' as a clever intellectual and inspiring speechmaker. Many of his ideas had influenced Lenin. However, he had only joined the Bolsheviks in 1917 and so not everyone trusted him. He had no loyal support base within the party and other potential leaders ganged up against him.

- Lenin had written in his 'testament' (his will) that Stalin was dangerous and should be removed from his position as General Secretary of the Party. However, Lenin had also said bad things about the other candidates for the leadership, so everyone agreed not to publish his views.

Top Tip

In 1924 few people regarded Stalin as the most likely to succeed Lenin. It was only later that they saw how powerful his position had been all along. This explains why the opportunity was not taken to stop him.

The Great Turn

- As a part of the struggle for power in the Communist Party between 1924 and 1929, there was a debate about the Russian (now called the Soviet) economy.

- The key question was, should the USSR be modernised by continuing with the New Economic Policy long term, or should industrialisation be accelerated, either in co-operation with other countries or through 'Socialism in one country'?

- Stalin positioned himself in the centre position in this debate, while his rivals for power cancelled each other out. In 1927 Trotsky was expelled from the Communist Party and later had to leave the country. By 1928 Stalin's only remaining rival was Nikolai Bukharin, with whom Stalin had devised the slogan 'Socialism in One Country'. Now Stalin would push Bukharin out by decisively rejecting the NEP and pushing for a radical '**Great Turn**' in the economy through **Collectivisation** and the **Five Year Plans**.

Quick Test

1. How did Stalin's positions in the Communist Party and government help him to become leader?

2. Why was Trotsky seen as the more likely successor?

3. Why did no one stop him replacing Lenin?

4. What new economic policies did Stalin support from 1928?

Did you hit your target for this topic? Give yourself a mark out of ten.

Answers 1. He was able to build up broad support across the Party. **2.** He was cleverer and a better speaker. **3.** They saw him as too dull and uninspiring to be a threat. **4.** Accelerated industrialisation within Russia alone.

Collectivisation and the Five Year Plans

Collectivisation

Collectivisation meant gathering all of the peasants that formed the majority of the Soviet population into large farms run by the government. This was the policy followed from 1929. There were several reasons for collectivisation:

- Property owners in the countryside were seen as the last remnants of Capitalism.

- Communists preferred a working class rather than peasant population. The working class were more likely to support the Communists. Collectivisation would turn peasants into workers because the collective farms would be like factories.

- In collective farms new methods and machinery like tractors could be introduced more easily to modernise farming.

- Collective farming would make it easier for the government to control food supply and distribution.

- The NEP was not providing enough surplus food to sell abroad to accelerate the growth of cities and industrialisation of Russia.

- There was resentment of **kulaks**, those peasants who were, it was believed, doing too well out of the NEP.

There were two types of collective farm; the **sovkhoz**, in which each peasant was paid a wage like a factory worker, and a **kolkhoz** in which each peasant had land to work on and any farm profits were distributed. By 1929 5 per cent of the USSR's farms had been collectivised. In that year Stalin announced that 25 per cent of farms would be collectivised within the year and then the rest would follow. This acceleration could not be achieved voluntarily.

- Collectivisation squads were sent out into the countryside to force collectivisation.

- Kulaks were identified and often killed, and their land and goods were handed to the new collective.

- There was resistance from peasants who did not want to lose independence. Crops and livestock were destroyed; the population of sheep and goats fell by two thirds, while the number of cows fell by over 40 per cent. Farm workers worked deliberately slowly.

- There were reports of cannibalism and a famine killed around 7 million people. This was kept secret at the time.

- Rationing and food shortages persisted well into the 1940s for tens of millions of Russians.

Top Tip

Sometimes peasants co-operated in collectivisation, accusing neighbours of being kulaks often out of jealousy. Others hoped that it might provide them with security. Look out for this in the sources.

- The kulaks were destroyed and agriculture was successfully brought under state control, with almost 100 per cent collectivisation by 1941. However the cost in human suffering was immeasurable.

MODERNISING RUSSIA

Five Year Plans

A key reason for collectivisation was to fund, feed and man rapid industrialisation in the Five Year Plans of the 1930s. There were several reasons for adopting a policy of rapid industrialisation:

- To provide for a modern industrialised army to match those of Germany, Britain, France and the USA.
- War with the west, in particular with Germany, seemed very likely.

The process was a remarkable, if very painful one:

- The economy was centrally planned through **GOSPLAN**, using quotas and target setting. The first plan from 1928 prioritised heavy industry; coal, iron and steel. The second plan prioritised tractors and other goods for collective farms. The third plan was overshadowed by the threat of war and focused on weapons.
- Large scale enterprises and factories were favoured. There was a huge hydro-electrical plant at Dnepropetrovsk, iron and steel works at Magnitogorsk, and huge canal projects.
- There was extensive use of slave labour through the system of **gulags** (labour camps).
- The secret police imposed strict discipline in factories.
- Over-achieving workers such as **Stakhanov** (a super human miner) were used to inspire workers.
- The process caused enormous suffering and was frequently very inefficient.

However, during the 1930s iron and steel production increased five-fold and coal production more than tripled. Industrialisation produced an economy and army capable of taking on and defeating the German Army in the Second World War.

Quick Test

1. What is meant by 'collectivisation'?
2. Why did the Communists want to collectivise Soviet farming?
3. What threat made the Communists introduce the Five Year Plans?
4. How successful were collectivisation and the Five Year Plans?

Did you hit your target for this topic? Give yourself a mark out of ten.

Answers 1. Bringing peasants together into large scale government owned farms **2.** They saw it as more modern; it would give them more control over the countryside; they thought it would turn capitalist peasants into communist workers. **3.** To compete with the threat from the modern industrialised armies in Capitalist countries **4.** Although inefficient and wasteful and although it caused incredible suffering, it provided the resources to take on Nazi Germany in 1941-45.

Purges

What were purges?

Purging (the expulsion of undesirable elements) and terror were both methods used by Lenin in the early 1920s to deal with opposition. In the 1930s, however, Stalin extended this on a scale previously unimagined, culminating in the **Great Terror** of 1936–38. The elimination of 'saboteurs', who were accused of holding up production, as well as the kulaks, was a part of this process, but there was also a political element that left no one safe.

Kirov

The main period of the Stalinist purges began with the murder in 1934 of **Kirov**, a popular Communist leader whose popularity with Communist Party workers appeared to rival Stalin's own status. Instead of being satisfied with the capture and execution of the man who killed Kirov, thousands more were implicated in the 'plot'. Many, including leading old Bolsheviks such as Kamenev and Zinoviev were expelled from the party, others were arrested and imprisoned.

Top Tip

Stalin may have been inspired by Hitler's **Night of the Long Knives** when he killed many of his own supporters and settled old scores. Ironically the purging of the army by Stalin left the Red Army much weakened and encouraged Hitler to invade in 1941.

Show trials

- From the middle of March 1934 it was decided that there should be public show trials to make examples of those found to be traitors to the revolution. 16 former colleagues of Stalin, including Kamenev and Zinoviev, were the first to publicly confess to crimes, many of which they could not possibly have committed, and be executed. This encouraged others to denounce 'traitors'.

- As time went on the net widened to take in more and more people, particularly once Yezhov became the enthusiastic head of the **NKVD** (the latest name for the secret police). Oddly, the higher in the hierarchy someone was, the more likely they were to be implicated and arrested. The former head of the NVKD, Yagoda, was one of those executed. People were encouraged to denounce colleagues and neighbours.

- The Great Terror accelerated significantly following the uncovering of the **Tukhachevsky Plot**. A hero of the civil war, Marshal Tukhachevsky, was a leading general and connections were found to his 'plot' that resulted in the elimination of around 35 000 officers from the Russian Army.

- Arrests were carried out by quota, and families and acquaintances of those accused were likely to be implicated and arrested also. The age at which the death penalty could be applied was lowered to 12.
- It was only in 1938 that Stalin decided that the Great Terror had gone too far. He had Yezhov arrested, thus bringing this phase of the purges to an end (although other purges continued right up to his death in 1953 and Trotsky was 'purged' by a man with an ice pick while in exile in Mexico in 1940).

Top Tip
The most frightening thing about the Stalinist purges was that even loyal Communists and supporters of Stalin were not free from arrest.

Gulags

Labour camps or gulags were an important part of the industrialisation effort of the 1930s. The NKVD would even do sweeps of public places, such as markets to arrest enough people to fill these camps. Since most of those arrested were never tried, these people simply vanished. If they were taken to a labour camp they could expect a horrendous journey in a cattle truck, pitiful rations and conditions, including temperatures well below freezing, and working hours that would ensure they literally worked to death.

It is not known how many people died in the Stalinist purges and gulags, but it is certainly a figure well into the millions and probably tens of millions.

Quick Test

1. Why might some people think that Stalin had Kirov killed?

2. Who was most enthusiastic in carrying out the purges?

3. Why was the arrest of Tukhachevsky a turning point?

4. What purpose was served by the gulags other than locking up Stalin's political opponents?

Did you hit your target for this topic? Give yourself a mark out of ten.

Answers 1. Stalin had cause to be jealous of Kirov and he was able to use his murder as an excuse to deal with his enemies. **2.** Yezhov **3.** It was the beginning of the purging of the Russian army that just weakened it just before the war. **4.** They helped with the industrialisation of Russia.

Enquiry skills

In **Source A**, Bukharin, a member of the Bolshevik Government, describes their White opponents.

> There can be no question of freedom for our opponents. The Bolshevik Party does not allow freedom of the press or freedom of speech for them. They are enemies of the people. The Party must ruthlessly put down all attempts by our white opponents to return to power. We alone maintain order.

1. What did Bukharin think of opponents of the Bolshevik Party?   3 marks

Source B is from *Russia 1914–41* by Colin Bagnall.

> As well as an inability to make progress in winning the war, the Provisional Government was unable effectively to tackle either the economic or social problems that had lain behind the protests of February 1917, or the new questions that were raised by the revolution. Inflation and food shortages got worse. Law and order were breaking down and peasants' demands for land reform grew more insistent

Top Tip
Here you are being asked about someone's opinion. You should try to say something about who they are and why they might say what is contained in the source. Link the reasons for his viewpoint to specific things that he has said about the Bolsheviks' opponents in this source.

2. How fully does Source B explain why the Provisional Government fell from power in October 1917? You must use the evidence from the source and your own knowledge and give reasons for your answer.

4 marks

Top Tip
In your answer you should quote the points that the author has made and include additional points from your own knowledge to give a complete account of the reasons for the Provisional Government's failure and a balanced answer to the question.

Source C is from Stalin's speech to the Communist Party Congress in 1927.

> *The way to improve agriculture is to turn the small and scattered peasant farms into large united farms based on the common cultivation of the land. The way ahead is to unite the small peasant farms gradually but surely, not by pressure but by example and persuasion, into large farms based on common, co-operative collective cultivation of the land. There is no other way to improve.*

3. Discuss Stalin's attitude towards agricultural change in Russia.   4 marks

You might answer this question like this:

"Stalin, the leader of the Soviet Union, was trying to persuade Party workers to support collectivisation. He suggests that bringing small farms together will make Russian agriculture more efficient. Interestingly at this point he supports using persuasion not pressure, possibly because, in 1927, he was not yet in a secure position, still engaged in a struggle for power. A more aggressive attitude towards the peasantry would not be popular with all in the Communist Party at that time. "

Note here that, although an attitude question and not requiring an evaluation of the source, referring to the date mentioned 'outside' the source is important to giving a full and balanced answer

Top Tip

Make sure that in 'attitude' questions like this you make it clear what side of the question the author is coming from and why. Use direct references to points made in the source to illustrate what you think the author's view is.

War, humiliation and the Treaty of Versailles

The end of the First World War and the overthrow of the Kaiser

After four years of war, by the late summer of 1918, it was clear to generals that Germany would lose the war. Allied troops had turned back the Spring Offensive, the Germans' last throw of the dice, and German troops were retreating across the front. Worse still, the German people were starved of food and resources by the British blockade. With labourers fighting at the front, Germany was producing less than half of its pre-war levels of meat and dairy goods. Over half a million Germans died from starvation and disease.

The fall of the **Kaiser** was due both to the actions of the generals and the actions of the German people:

- The generals wanted to avoid responsibility for losing the war.
- They also hoped that the democratic countries, Britain, France and the USA, would offer better terms to a **democratic** German government than to a **dictatorship** under the Kaiser.
- The allies refused to negotiate until Germany got rid of the Kaiser.
- On 25 October a mutiny broke out at the naval base in **Kiel** to prevent the navy going to sea.
- In the following week strikes and demonstrations spread across Germany. In some areas councils (like the soviets that had appeared in Russia immediately before the 1917 Revolution) were set up. Revolution looked likely in Germany too.
- Moderate socialists, the **Social Democrats** were the biggest party in the German Parliament (the **Reichstag**). They wanted to prevent a revolution and end the war. On 7 November, their leader, Ebert, declared that the Kaiser must abdicate.
- The Chancellor (German Prime Minister) Prince Max announced the abdication of the Kaiser. The next day the Kaiser fled to Holland.
- An **armistice** (ceasefire) was signed between Germany and the allies on 11 November 1918.

Top Tip
Between 1918 and 1933 a lot of events occurred that explain the rise to power of the Nazis. This would be a good time to start a timeline adding key events as you go through the next few units.

Unit IIID: Germany, 1918–1939

The Treaty of Versailles

In June 1919 the allies met in Versailles on the outskirts of Paris to decide the fate of Germany. The resulting treaty was much harsher than the Germans had anticipated.

- The Germans had replaced the Kaiser with a democratic government as the allies wanted.
- Woodrow Wilson had declared that his '**14 points**' would be the basis of a fair treaty.
- Most Germans believed that no one country could be blamed for the war.

There were five reasons why the Germans felt bitterly disappointed by the treaty:

- The **War Guilt Clause** of the treaty blamed Germany alone for the war and forced them to pay reparations.
- It was a 'dictated peace' (**diktat**) as the German delegation was not consulted.
- Germany was split in two by the '**Polish Corridor**'.
- There were Germans left outside Germany.
- The German armed forces were left deliberately weak.

There was outrage in the German press. The Germans who were forced to sign the treaty came to be called **November Criminals** (because the armistice had been signed in November). This made it very difficult for the new government to win support in Germany.

Top Tip

To identify German reactions, write some headlines that might have appeared in German newspapers on 29 June, the day after the treaty was signed.

Quick Test

1. Why did the German generals believe that the Kaiser should go?
2. Why was it feared that there would be a revolution in Germany?
3. Why did the Germans believe that the treaty would not be a harsh one?
4. What was the connection between the War Guilt Clause and the payment of reparations?

Did you hit your target for this topic? Give yourself a mark out of ten.

Answers 1. They hoped that democratic countries would give better terms to a democratic Germany and that they would not be blamed for defeat. **2.** The people were hungry and desperate and strikes and mutinies had spread across the country. **3.** The Kaiser had abdicated and Woodrow Wilson had put forward proposals for a fair treaty. **4.** The War Guilt Clause justified the payment of reparations.

The Weimar Republic: a new start?

In January 1919 the German people elected a new **National Assembly**. Because of violence in Berlin, they met in the provincial town of Weimar. The town gave its name to the new Republic (a state with no king or queen).

The Weimar Constitution

The National Assembly drew up a new Constitution for the new Republic. It was widely regarded as the most democratic in the world:

- A **President** would be elected every seven years.
- A **Chancellor**, supported by a majority in the Reichstag, would be chosen by the President.
- The **Reichstag** would be elected by the population according to **Proportional Representation**. That is, the seats for each party in the Reichstag would exactly reflect the number of votes each party had won in the election. This is different from national elections in Britain and America, where the system gives many extra seats to the biggest parties.
- The basic rights of all Germans were embedded in the Constitution, including the right to vote, to freedom of movement provided no law is broken, freedom of expression, to meet in groups, to join trade unions and to own their own property.
- Under **Article 48** of the Constitution, the President could declare a national emergency and suspend many of the terms of the Constitution, ruling as a temporary dictator.

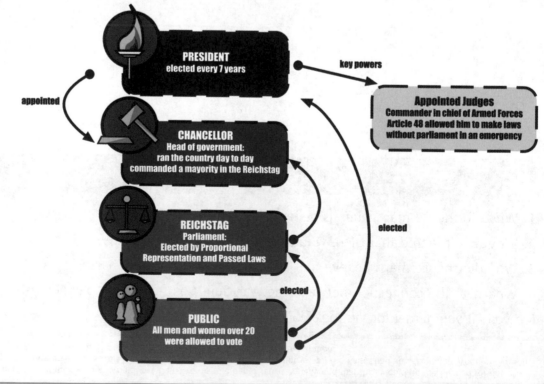

PRESIDENT
elected every 7 years

key powers

appointed

Appointed Judges
Commander in chief of Armed Forces
Article 48 allowed him to make laws
without parliament in an emergency

CHANCELLOR
Head of government:
ran the country day to day
commanded a mayority in the Reichstag

REICHSTAG
Parliament:
Elected by Proportional
Representation and Passed Laws

elected

PUBLIC
All men and women over 20
were allowed to vote

elected

Problems facing the Weimar Republic

- The first things that the new Republic had to do were to sign the armistice and agree to the 'diktat' of the Treaty of Versailles. It was therefore tainted with failure and humiliation from the start.

- The generals not only successfully avoided blame for losing the war, but a myth began to spread that the German Army had not in fact been defeated at all, but had instead been 'stabbed in the back' by politicians who had betrayed Germany. The German word for this myth was the **dolchstoss**.

- Although the Reichstag had existed for some time, there was not a long tradition of party democracy in Germany. Many Germans preferred to trust military men who they saw as straightforward rather than politicians.

- The Treaty of Versailles had taken important industrial territory away from Germany and imposed heavy **reparations** of £6.6 billion which they had to start paying from the early 1920s.

- Proportional Representation allowed small and extremist parties to gain a foothold in the Reichstag and establish a base upon which they could attack the Republic itself. The rights guaranteed under the Constitution made it difficult for the Republic to defend itself.

- The President had a lot of power and could be a potential dictator.

- Many civil servants, judges and Nationalist and Communist politicians were hostile to the very idea of a democratic republic like Weimar.

- The Republic had to deal with a series of political and economic crises in the first five years that made it difficult for it to establish itself.

Top Tip
All of the above problems are important, but perhaps not all equally so. Try to create a hierarchy of causes from the most dangerous and difficult to the least important.

Quick Test

1. What powers did the President have and why might these be dangerous?

2. What basic rights did German citizens have under the Constitution?

3. How did the Treaty of Versailles undermine the Weimar Republic? Give three reasons.

4. Why might the voting system of proportional representation have caused problems for the Republic?

Did you hit your target for this topic? Give yourself a mark out of ten.

Answers 1. He could suspend the constitution in an emergency – this would make him a dictator if he wanted to be. **2.** The right to vote, freedom of speech and expression, property ownership and trade union membership. **3.** It linked the new government to the humiliation of losing the war; it crippled Germany economically and made it difficult for the new government to rebuild the country; it created the myth of the dolchstoss – that politicians had stabbed the army in the back. **4.** It meant that elected governments were coalitions, potentially unstable and it allowed extremist parties to get a foothold.

Revolts

In the first five years of its existence, the Weimar Republic faced serious opposition from groups that wanted to destroy the new German democracy.

The Spartacists and the Kapp Putsch

- In January 1919 left-wing revolutionaries called **Spartacists**, led by **Karl Liebknecht** and **Rosa Luxemburg** tried to overthrow Ebert's new government to set up a Communist state like the USSR in which the government took over all industry and land.

- Demonstrations across Germany had been building since December 1918, with demands for power to be handed to the Workers' and Soldiers' Councils. They captured newspaper offices and railway stations in Berlin.

- In November, Ebert made an agreement with the leading general, **Groener**, that he would not interfere in the running of the army if the army supported the government.

- The Spartacist Rising was easily put down by **Freikorps**, ex-soldiers organised by Groener to restore order, killing over 100 Spartacists. The government now seemed to be in the hands of the army.

- Under the terms of the Treaty of Versailles the German Army had to be reduced to 100 000 men. The expelled soldiers joined the freikorps, which the allies saw as an alternative army. The government came under pressure to disband the freikorps.

- In March 1920 some of the freikorps led by **Wolfgang Kapp** took control of Berlin in a **Putsch** (an attempt to take over the government by force) and declared a national government. Ebert's government was forced to flee.

- Ebert's government received no help from the army and instead appealed to the workers for help. Trade unions organised a general strike that paralysed the Putsch.

- The leaders of the Putsch were not punished.

Top Tip
A large number of names of individuals and organisations appear in this unit. It might be a good idea to put together your own glossary as you go along.

The Spartacist revolt and Kapp putsch both attacked Weimar's coalition governments.

The Munich Putsch

In 1923 the Weimar Republic faced its greatest crisis yet; French occupation and **hyperinflation**. Someone who was prepared to take advantage of this crisis was **Adolf Hitler**, leader of a small political party called the **Nazis**.

- Together with the paramilitary **Sturm Abteilung** (SA) and the support of the hero of the First World War, **General Ludendorff**, the Nazis planned to launch a **Putsch**.

- Germany was divided into regions, called **Länder**, each of which had its own government. The plan was to take over the government of Bavaria first and use it as the base for a march on Berlin. In doing this Hitler was copying the Italian Fascist leader, Mussolini, who had gained support for his overthrow of the democratic government in Italy in 1922 by marching on Rome.

- In November Hitler and his supporters tried to take over a meeting in a beer hall organised by the popular nationalist **von Kahr**. However, it was poorly planned. Some of Hitler's men under the command of **Ernst Röhm** were trapped in government buildings, and Hitler and the SA marched to the rescue. They were ambushed, leading to the death of 16 Nazis and three policemen.

- Hitler and Ludendorff were put on trial. This turned out to be a wonderful opportunity for Hitler who turned the trial into a platform for him to tell the whole country about himself and his ideas.

- Hitler was given the minimum possible sentence by a sympathetic judge; 5 years. He only served 8 months. Ludendorff was allowed to go free entirely.

Quick Test

1. Who were the Spartacists and what did they want?

2. What was the Kapp Putsch?

3. Who were the two main leaders of the Munich Putsch?

4. How did the trial after Munich actually help Hitler?

Did you hit your target for this topic? Give yourself a mark out of ten.

Answers 1. They were communists who wanted to start a revolution in Germany and overthrow the government. **2.** An attempt by ex-soldiers in the Freikorps to take over the government. **3.** Adolf Hitler and General Ludendorff **4.** It made him famous across Germany.

Hyperinflation

How did hyperinflation come about?

As well as rebuilding Germany after the devastation of war, the government had to deal with the problems created by the Treaty of Versailles. The government did not keep up its payments of reparations to France and Belgium. These two countries' governments quickly lost patience with the Germans and marched into the Ruhr region of Germany in January 1923, as the treaty gave them the right to do. This was the most industrialised part of Germany and the French and Belgians intended forcing coal and industrial goods to be loaded onto trains and taken as reparations. The German Government appealed for **passive resistance**, i.e. ignoring the French and Belgians and refusing to do any work. This had two effects:

- There was a sharp decline in how much was produced in Germany. This created shortages, meaning that prices rapidly increased. This is called **inflation**.

- The government met the high cost of paying striking workers by simply printing more money. So much money was printed that it quickly became worth very little. This caused **hyperinflation**.

What was the impact of hyperinflation?

The effects of hyperinflation were disastrous:

- In 1922 1 US$ could be purchased for 400 **Deutschmarks** (DM); by February 1923 it cost 7000 DM, by August it cost 1 million DM, and by November it cost 130 billion DM.

- Anyone who lived on savings or a pension had their income wiped out overnight. Those with salaries, such as teachers or doctors found that their salaries also quickly became worth very little.

- Prices went up several times a day, so workers had to be paid several times a day and spend their wages immediately.

- Those with land or property which they did not sell were fine, and some businessmen were even able to make profit out of the situation. The very poor had little to lose in any case. The middle classes lost the most and were quick to blame the Weimar Government for their unaccustomed poverty.

Top Tip

It is important to realise that events did not impact on everyone the same way. Try putting yourself in the shoes of a factory worker, a pensioner, a teacher, an unemployed person and a businessman. Write a short 'speech bubble' for each explaining how hyperinflation affected them.

How did Germany recover from hyperinflation?

The German Chancellor from August 1923 **Gustav Stresemann** took firm action to end the crisis.

- Left wing governments in some German cities were deposed to satisfy the right wing generals.
- Passive resistance was called off.
- The US banker **Charles Dawes** was called in to renegotiate the payment of reparations and arrange loans from **Wall Street** (New York's stock exchange) to rebuild German industry and trade. This was called the **Dawes Plan**.
- The Deutschmark was abolished and notes burned and replaced with a new, more credible currency, the **Rentenmark**, which in turn was replaced with the even more secure **Reichsmark**.
- Stresemann worked to improve relations with other countries, negotiating the **Locarno Treaty** in 1925 and joining the **League of Nations**.
- Between 1924 and 1929 there was a period of stability and relative prosperity in Germany.

Top Tip
The changes made to help Germany recover all seem very positive. However, underlying problems that you already know about still existed. Think about what they might be.

Quick Test

1. What part of Germany did French and Belgian troops occupy in 1923?
2. How did the German government respond to this action?
3. What is hyperinflation and who was worst affected by the German hyperinflation of 1923?
4. What happened to the German currency to bring hyperinflation to an end? In what other ways did Stresemann help to make Germany more stable?

Did you hit your target for this topic? Give yourself a mark out of ten.

Answers 1. They invaded the Ruhr. **2.** It was called for a policy of passive resistance. **3.** Hyperinflation is when prices rise very rapidly; those with savings and fixed incomes were worst affected. **4.** A new currency was introduced and Stresemann negotiated loans with the American banker Dawes, who helped reorganise the payment of reparations. Stresemann also established better relations with other European countries.

Depression

What was the impact of the Depression on German people?

In October 1929 the stock market on **Wall Street** collapsed. This was called the **Wall Street Crash**. As the price of shares in US companies fell rapidly and people lost fortunes, those who had loaned money to German businesses demanded their money back. All over the world those who traded with the USA had to close down businesses, and few had the money to buy things, creating a knock on effect around the world called the **Great Depression**. Because of the loans organised under the **Dawes Plan**, however, Germany was the country worst affected.

In Germany:

- businesses closed
- unemployment increased from just over 1 million in 1928 to 3 million in 1930 and almost 6 million in 1932: 40 per cent of all factory workers were unemployed
- the government raised taxes and cut **unemployment benefits** to try to save money. This made conditions even more extreme for many Germans.
- hunger and homelessness was widespread.

Top Tip

A common mistake for candidates is to confuse the Depression after 1929 with the hyperinflation of 1923 because they were both economic crises. However the Depression was actually the opposite of hyperinflation (prices go down in a depression) and it affected different people.

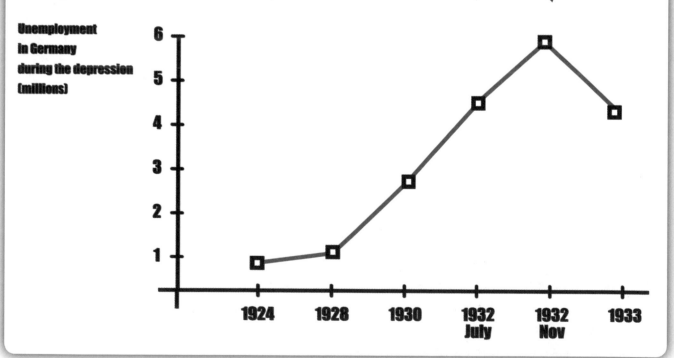

Unemployment in Germany during the depression (millions)

How did the Depression make the Weimar Republic weaker?

The German Government was no more able than the governments of Britain, France or America to deal with the Depression. Printing more money and spending it to get people back to work was impossible because of fear that it might lead to a repeat of the hyperinflation of 1923. Instead, taxes were raised and spending was cut, making matters worse for most Germans.

As governments failed to deal with the crisis, President Hindenburg turned to the emergency clause, Article 48, that allowed him to rule as a dictator by presidential decree. Democracy in Germany was therefore weakened.

As they became more desperate, voters began to listen to more extreme parties that were hostile to the Republic and offered radical alternatives. In particular they turned to the Communists and the Nazis, whose support in the Reichstag began to grow.

Top Tip
The Wall Street Crash is another great subject for a ripple diagram. Write 'Wall Street Crash' in the middle of a blank sheet of paper. Draw the consequences of the crash in concentric circles moving from the most immediate on the inside to the least immediate on the outside.

Quick Test

1. What was the Wall Street Crash and why was Germany more seriously affected than most countries?

2. How many Germans were unemployed by 1932? How did the government respond to the crisis?

3. Who was the president of Germany during the Great Depression?

4. What was Article 48 of the constitution and what did it do to German democracy?

Did you hit your target for this topic? Give yourself a mark out of ten.

Answers 1. The Wall Street Crash was the dramatic loss in the value of shares on the American stock exchange. When American investors needed money they recalled the loans that they had made to German industry under the Dawes Plan. **2.** 6 Million. The government tried to save money by cutting unemployment benefits, creating even more misery. **3.** Hindenburg. **4.** It allowed the President to rule without the Reichstag (Parliament) and it turned Germany into a virtual dictatorship during the crisis of the Depression.

The rise of the Nazis

Origins and organisation

The **National Socialist Workers' Party** (NSDAP) was founded in 1919 as the German Workers' Party by Anton Drexler. They were nicknamed the **Nazis** because of the sound of the first two words of their name in German.

- The party was quickly taken over by army veteran **Adolf Hitler**.

- It was one of a number of small right wing parties that had emerged at the end of the war. They had similar ideas about the Treaty of Versailles, belief in the dolchstoss, **anti-semitic** views (hatred of Jews) and the need for strong government. However, what made the Nazis stand out was the ability of Hitler to motivate crowds through his speeches.

- At first the Nazis, based mainly in **Bavaria** tried to take power by force in the Munich Putsch.

- The trial in Munich made Hitler a nationally known figure for the first time.

- In prison, Hitler dictated his memoirs, *Mein Kampf* (My Struggle), to **Rudolf Hess** and re-thought the Nazi's approach to taking power.

- The Nazi party was re-organised as a national party that could win votes across the whole of Germany. Each district was led by a 'gauleiter' who was supposed to be a little **führer** (leader) who based himself on Hitler's example. This would help them mobilise support later.

- They adopted the distinctive **swastika**, the red, black and white Nazi flag.

- The SA, dressed in military uniforms, intimidated trade unionists, Socialists and Communists.

Top Tip
The key causes of Nazi success were Hitler and the Depression. Think of three reasons why each was important then put them in rank order.

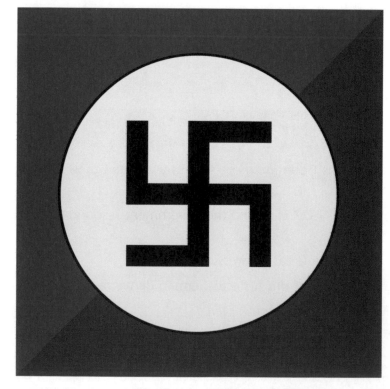

Getting into power

The Nazis had little success while Germany was stable and prosperous. In 1928, the Nazis had just 12 seats in the Reichstag and Hitler was widely regarded as irrelevant.

- The impact of the Wall Street Crash and the Depression on Nazi fortunes was felt almost immediately. By 1930 Nazi support had increased to over 6 million votes (100 seats).
- The Nazis were able to take advantage of the situation and build on their success.
- They appeared to offer an end to unemployment and popular opposition to the Treaty of Versailles.
- They exploited fear of Communism among the middle class, farmers and industrialists.
- Propaganda was used to promote Hitler as a messiah. The novelty of air travel was used to ensure that he could speak at as many mass rallies as possible.
- The SA used violence on the streets to stir up an image of chaos which Hitler claimed only the strong and military-looking Nazis could solve.

By July 1932 the Nazis were the largest single party with 230 seats and Hitler had become a respectable second to Hindenburg in the Presidential elections, winning 13 million votes.

The economy was beginning to recover under the policies of Chancellor **Brüning** and it looked like Hitler's moment had passed. In new elections in November the Nazi vote fell by 34 seats.

However, the Nazis were rescued. After a failed attempt by **von Schleicher** to split the Nazi Party, in January 1933 **von Papen** managed to persuade Hitler to become Chancellor in a government containing three Nazis and leading members of other nationalist parties. Papen thought that he could control Hitler and the apparently weakening Nazi Party. He was wrong.

Top Tip

Nazi fortunes went down as well as up between 1920 and 1933. Draw a graph to show how Nazi fortunes fluctuated. Try to explain the turning points.

Quick Test

1. How did Hitler use his time in prison?
2. What was Hitler's great strength as a leader?
3. How did the Depression affect Nazi support?
4. Why did it appear Hitler's moment had passed in November 1932? What rescued him?

Did you hit your target for this topic? Give yourself a mark out of ten.

Answers 1. He wrote Mein Kampf **2.** Speechmaking **3.** They gained a lot more support. **4.** Support for the Nazis declined – but they were saved by von Papen offering him a place in government.

Nazi Government

The Reichstag fire and the Enabling Act

In January 1933 Hitler was outnumbered in the government by non-Nazis. His first objective was to establish sole Nazi control over the government.

The President, Hindenburg, although by now a very old man, remained extremely suspicious of Hitler. He disliked his professed hatred for the Jews, for whom Hindenburg had respect, and he was dismissive of the humble roots of this 'jumped up little corporal'. He had only agreed to appoint Hitler as Chancellor after a great deal of persuasion by von Papen and in the face of the immense crisis of the depression.

- A new election was called for **5 March 1933** to try to get an absolute majority in the Reichstag. Their main opponents were the Social Democrats and the Communists.

- On 27 February the Nazis had an incredible stroke of luck. The Reichstag was burned down by a young Dutch anarchist **Marinus Van der Lubbe** who wanted to start a revolution. Those accused of plotting with him were later acquitted, but the Nazis were quick to declare this as the start of the Communist revolution.

- Hitler persuaded Hindenburg to use **Article 48** to declare a state of emergency. The SA and police rounded up Communists and shut down opposition newspapers. The Nazis won 288 seats (44 per cent of the vote). 81 Communists won seats, but they were not allowed into the Reichstag.

- Still needing a two thirds majority to change the Constitution and create a dictatorship, Hitler used the threat of Communist revolution and intimidation by the SA and the **SS (Schutz-Staffel)** (Hitler's elite bodyguard) to persuade all except for the 94 Social Democrats in the Reichstag to support an **Enabling Act** that gave the Chancellor sweeping personal powers.

Top Tip

There is a lot of debate about whether Van der Lubbe did start the fire alone or whether it was secretly started by the Nazis, who benefited most from it. There is no right answer to this. The key thing to remember is how the Nazis were able to take advantage of this event to consolidate power

Establishing the dictatorship

The Enabling Act was used to establish a Nazi dictatorship.

- The Communists were banned in May, the Social Democrats were banned in June. In July all parties except for the Nazis were banned and only Nazi candidates could stand for office. Trade unions were also banned

- All that stood in Hitler's way now was the army. The army remained suspicious. The members of the SA, led by **Ernst Röhm**, were radical and brutal hooligans, and saw themselves as the army of the new Germany and wanted to replace the army. Generals were also concerned that the SA broke the limit of 100 000 set on the German Army by the Treaty of Versailles and invited invasion by France.

- The head of the SS, **Heinrich Himmler** organised the brutal **Night of the Long Knives** (30 June – 1 July 1934) in which leading members of the SA (including Röhm) were murdered along with those who had crossed Hitler such as von Streicher and Strasser.

- When Hindenburg died in 1935, Hitler was able to declare himself **Führer**, sole dictator of Germany with the full support of the army. All members of the army swore allegiance to Adolf Hitler personally. The Nazis now set about consolidating a **police state**.

Top Tip

To keep clear in your mind how Hitler was able to establish himself as dictator of Germany try to think of a way of representing how he overcame the obstacles to power. Perhaps you could use labelled bricks or blocks in a wall to represent the obstacles and write down the method Hitler used to remove each one.

Quick Test

1. Why did the Nazis call a new election for March 1933?

2. Name three things the Nazis did to exploit the Reichstag fire.

3. Which was the only party to vote against the Enabling Act?

4. Why was the army pleased by the Night of the Long Knives?

Did you hit your target for this topic? Give yourself a mark out of ten.

Answers 1. To try to get a majority in the Reichstag **2.** They pushed for a state of Emergency to be declared; locked up opposition leaders; shut down newspapers; passed the Enabling Act. **3.** The Social Democrats **4.** It got rid of the SA and Röhm who were trying to take over control of the army

The Nazis in power 1: the treatment of Jews

Nazi ideas about race

Hitler wrote down his ideas in *Mein Kampf*. These included overthrowing the Treaty of Versailles, rebuilding the German Army and creating 'living space' (**Lebensraum**) in eastern Europe by wars of expansion that would eventually destroy Soviet Communism. However, the most important theme running through the book was race.

- Hitler believed that humanity was divided into a racial hierarchy.
- At the top of Hitler's hierarchy were **Aryans**, the master race, represented by the people of Germany and Scandinavia. He believed they were destined to rule over inferior races, such as the 'Slavs' to the East.
- Hitler believed that the Nazis had to 'purify' the German people by eliminating those he despised; criminals, the disabled and homosexuals, amongst many others.
- Some groups he even called '**untermenschen**' (sub-humans).
- Hitler reserved his greatest contempt for Jews and gypsies. The Jews were accused of causing defeat in the First World War, of creating Communism, of being ruthless Capitalists and bankers who had brought about economic problems, and of systematically undermining German strength.

Anti-Semitism (hatred of Jews) was not new in Europe. Persecution of Jews began when Christian soldiers had murdered and robbed from Jews on their way to **the First Crusade** in 1096. The Russian Tsar carried out **pogroms** (systematic attacks) on Jews, and in Britain, cartoons and newspaper articles attacked Jews living in London.

Jews living in Germany, often for many generations, and many non-Jewish Germans did not see German Jews as any less German than the rest of the population. Changing this idea was Hitler's first task in carrying out the **persecution** of Jews in Germany.

Top Tip

Unlike much previous persecution of the Jews, Hitler's ideas were solely racist rather than religious. It is less important to understand why he believed these things than to understand that his ideas about purity of the master race underpinned all of his other policies. Look out for this as you look at his other actions in Germany.

How were Jews treated in Germany in the 1930s?

- In 1933 the SA led a **boycott** of Jewish businesses, smashing shop windows and burning Jewish books on huge bonfires.

- Jews lost their jobs in the professions and the army.

- Because many Germans seemed unenthusiastic, a huge effort was put into anti-Jewish **propaganda**; posters, films, newspapers, even children's games and colouring books portrayed Aryan Germans as good, strong and pure, and Jews as dirty, dishonest and dangerous. The school curriculum reinforced these ideas.

- Jews were encouraged to emigrate, but they were not allowed to take their property with them. Most chose to ride out the storm of Nazism as in previous persecutions.

- The **Nuremburg Laws** of September 1935 removed German Citizenship from Jews. Jews now had no rights in society. They were socially separated from other Germans by outlawing marriage and sexual relations between Jews and non-Jews.

- A speech by Hitler in September 1937 marked a rapid acceleration of persecution as more Jewish businesses were confiscated, doctors, dentists and lawyers were not allowed to have Aryan clients, and Jews had to have a red 'J' stamped on their passports.

- On 9–10 November 1938, the SS organised the destruction of Jewish synagogues, homes and shops across Germany. This was called **Kristallnacht**. Hundreds of Jews were killed or imprisoned in concentration camps. Within a year Germany would be at war and this process would lead to the **genocide** across Europe known as **the Holocaust**.

Top Tip

The most important thing Hitler wanted to do was to convince most Germans that Jews could not also be Germans. Look out for the ways in which he did this.

Quick Test

1. Where did Hitler write down his ideas about race? Who were the Aryans? What were Hitler's accusations about the Jews?

2. What actions did the SA carry out in 1933?

3. How was persecution of the Jews stepped up in 1935?

4. What happened on Kristallnacht?

Did you hit your target for this topic? Give yourself a mark out of ten.

Answers 1. Hitler wrote about race in Mein Kampf; he claimed that the Aryans (Germans and Nordic peoples) were superior; he blamed the Jews for the loss of the War, Communism, the Treaty of Versailles and the Great Depression. **2.** They organised boycott of Jewish owned shops. **3.** The Nuremburg Laws were passed. **4.** Synagogues, Jewish homes and businesses were destroyed by the SS; hundreds were killed or arrested.

The Nazis in power 2: young people

The importance of the young

Young people were particularly important to the Nazis. Most adults had made up their minds about the new Germany, but young people could still be persuaded and were the future of the **Third Reich** (this is what Hitler called the Nazi regime). They were also the generation that would be involved in the wars that Hitler expected to be a part of the expansion of Germany. Great care was taken in indoctrinating children with Nazi ideas.

The Hitler Youth

The Hitler Youth was set up in 1925, and once the Nazis came to power its membership rose substantially, at first through its promotion by the government, then by compulsion.

- There were organisations for boys: the '**Pimpf**' for those 6–10, the **Deutsche Jungvolk** for those 10–14 and the **Hitler Jugend** (**Hitler Youth**) for those 14–18.

- There were separate organisations for girls: the **Jungmadel** for those up to 14 and the **Bund Deutscher Madel** (**League of German Maidens**) for those 14–21.

- Many boys enjoyed the uniforms, the outdoor activities, parades, model making, competitions and sports that were central to the Hitler Youth. They were also taught about mythical customs for burial of the dead, amongst other things.

- Children were encouraged to inform on their parents and friends. Adults were afraid to interfere in the Hitler Youth.

- There was also indoctrination of all members of youth organisations into Nazi ideas, through reading of **Der Stürmer** and study of Hitler's speeches.

- Girls were kept separate, but did very similar activities to the boys even though they were not being trained to fight. They were also trained to make beds and conduct first aid.

- Once these organisations became compulsory, however, enthusiasm for the youth organisations declined. Drilling became more central to their activities and games less important.

Top Tip
Remember the purpose of the Hitler Youth was to train boys and girls for the challenges of war to come. Try to find five ways in which youth organisations did this by using library resources or the Internet.

Education

- All teachers who refused to join the **National Socialist Teachers' League** were sacked.
- The **National Curriculum** and **textbooks** were rewritten by the Nazis.
- German language and History emphasised the greatness of Germany and betrayal of Germany by other nations, such as the French. Biology taught **eugenics** (the differences between races).
- In addition, new subjects such as **Ideology** and **Race studies** were introduced.
- Geography, Chemistry and Mathematics emphasised military aspects also, with examples put into military contexts (e.g. questions about the bomb loads of German aircraft).
- Girls were taught motherhood and home craft.
- Jews were picked on and humiliated by Nazi teachers and eventually removed from mainstream schools. In Jewish schools subjects were geared to preparing children for emigration.

Top Tip
Not all young people felt the same about youth movements and Nazi education. Some were enthusiastic, particularly about the youth movements, but others disliked them, even if they weren't excluded.

Quick Test

1. Why were young people especially important to the Nazis?

2. What were the main Nazi Youth organisations?

3. Why did the youth organisations become less popular?

4. How did the Nazis make sure that teachers taught Nazi ideas?

Did you hit your target for this topic? Give yourself a mark out of ten.

Answers 1. They were more easily influenced; they represented the future and would be the soldiers in a future war. **2.** The Pimpf, the Hitler Youth and the League of German Maidens. **3.** They became compulsory and there were fewer games and more drilling. **4.** Non-Nazi teachers were sacked; Nazi textbooks and curricula were issued.

The Nazis in power 3: militarism and intimidation

The police state

Nazi Germany was a **dictatorship**. The militarism of soldiers and Nazi Party members parading in mass rallies often in specially built stadiums gave an impression that everything was very well organised. Hitler as Führer was in ultimate control. However, he only worked for a few hours per day and left the drudgery of running the government to other people. So who did run Germany?

- The **SA** led the intimidation of enemies or threats to the Nazis, until, following the **Night of the Long Knives**, the SA came under the control of the SS.

- The **SS** were Hitler's bodyguard, but under the leadership of **Heinrich Himmler** had supplanted the SA and became the most important arm of the police state.

- Under SS control was the **Gestapo**, the secret police most feared by Nazi opposition. They used informers, read mail and tapped phones. Anyone suspected of any opposition could be arrested.

- **Spies and informers** in each residential block and each workplace, even within families, ensured that no one could speak out or organise against the regime.

- The SS also ran the **concentration camps** that were set up across Germany. The first one was opened in **Dachau** near Munich in 1933. In these camps of huts surrounded by barbed wire fences were imprisoned those of whom the regime disapproved. Members of trade unions, opposition parties, Jews, homosexuals and those who told jokes about the regime were all liable to find themselves in a concentration camp. There they had no rights and would be subject to hard labour and mistreatment by the SS guards. Fear of being put in one intimidated those opposed to or indifferent to the Nazis.

- The legal system was **arbitrary** (worked in an unpredictable way). Nazi judges were appointed and the legal code was changed to make anything the Nazi leadership might consider inappropriate illegal.

Top Tip

The fact that the Nazi Government was not as well organised as it portrayed itself in propaganda did not make it any less frightening. In fact quite the opposite, since there was no way of ensuring that you were safe from arrest.

How did people react to Nazi Government?

The Nazis had two main demands of the German people in the 1930s: to obey without question and to prepare for war.

Propaganda, under the control of **Josef Goebbels**, was used to reinforce the ideals of Nazism. Films such as those by Leni Riefenstahl attacked Jews and foreigners and glorified the achievements of the Third Reich. Military parades and rallies were designed to make Germans feel strong and proud of their military traditions. Posters with slogans, such as '**One People! One Reich! One Führer!**' shouted out unity and obedience. Radios that could only tune into official Nazi channels were made easily available, and all work stopped during Hitler's broadcasts.

Although fear was an important factor in preventing Germans from opposing the regime, Germans who were not Jewish, not Socialists, not Communists, not disabled or who did not have a disabled relative, felt relatively prosperous and they often approved of, or did not strongly object to the regime. Thanks largely to the Nazi policies of **rearming** and the reintroduction of **conscription** in the mid-1930s, as well as dismissing 'undesirables' from many jobs, unemployment fell. The Nazis also carried out large scale building projects, most famously the **autobahns**, the first motorways. Provision was made for holiday camps for many ordinary Germans under the '**Strength through Joy**' programme. The success of Hitler's foreign policy up to 1938 also won the Nazis popularity.

ONE PEOPLE! ONE REICH! ONE FÜHRER!

Top Tip

In recent years historians have emphasised the extent to which many ordinary Germans collaborated with the Nazi regime. There were relatively few Gestapo officers in each town, but there were those who would inform on their neighbours out of jealousy, prejudice or malice, not only from fear.

Quick Test

1. Which organisation was controlled by Heinrich Himmler?
2. What was the Gestapo and why were Germans afraid to speak out against the regime?
3. Who did the Nazis put into concentration camps?
4. Why did many Germans support the Nazi Government in the 1930s?

Did you hit your target for this topic? Give yourself a mark out of ten.

Answers 1. The SS. **2.** The Secret Police: those that spoke out were arrested. **3.** Political opponents; trade unionists; Jews; homosexuals. **4** Most Germans felt economically better off than before; foreign policy was successful until 1939

Opposition

How did ordinary Germans oppose the Nazis?

- Because of fear of the police state, and because increasing numbers supported the Nazis in the 1930s, opposition to the Nazis was extremely difficult.

- Many Germans could claim that they did not know much of what was happening due to censorship and propaganda, while the Nazis could claim that they had come to power legally through elections.

- The opposition was divided. The largest political opponents of the Nazis were the Social Democrats and Communists, but they had not worked together before they were banned and did not work together once the dictatorship was imposed.

- There were no attempts to overthrow the Nazis until the very end of the war. Having taken a personal oath to Hitler, members of the army, the only people who could realistically succeed in overthrowing the regime, felt bound by loyalty.

- There was some passive resistance to Nazism. Many risked imprisonment or even execution by attending secret Socialist Party meetings, refusing to join the Nazi Party or refusing to salute.

- Once war broke out some young people formed groups called the **Edelweiss Pirates** and the **White Rose** group. They organised festivals of 'swing' music, a form of jazz condemned by the Nazis, and accepted Jews into their groups, even helping deserters and camp escapees and distributing leaflets. Many members of these groups were condemned to concentration camps or executed.

Top Tip

Try writing a short essay on resistance to Nazism. Include an introduction that sets the topic in context, e.g. why it was difficult to resist, then give five points, each one fully explained.

"Arbeit Macht Frei" is German for "Work makes one free"

The churches

Once the army had been appeased by the **Night of the Long Knives** and swore their oath of loyalty to Hitler, the largest independent bodies not under Nazi control were the Christian churches. Although Hitler despised Christianity, the churches were difficult for the Nazis to deal with because of the chaos of Nazi organisation in practice and because many Nazis were churchgoers.

In the 1939 Census over 44 million Germans (the vast majority) stated that they were Christians. In some local areas, the Nazi leadership arrested priests and ministers, in others the local Nazi leaders were leading members of the congregation.

- In 1940 the programme of **euthanasia** (murdering the disabled) was ended in Germany because of protests by the churches and the appeals of bereaved relatives.

- Some ministers and priests, such as Martin Niemoller, Paul Schneider, Cardinal Van Galen and Dietrich Bonhoeffer attacked Nazism in sermons. Some were imprisoned in concentration camps and executed, a few were left alone.

- Jehovah's witnesses often refused to conform to Nazi wishes and 10 000 died in concentration camps.

Only a minority, even in the church, openly resisted Nazism. The Catholic Church signed a **Concordat** with Hitler in 1933 agreeing to work with the new regime. After 1935 the Nazis took firmer action against the churches, setting up a **Department of Church Affairs** to monitor them, arresting ministers who opposed the regime, harassing church schools and youth movements and banning carols, nativity plays and Religious Education lessons from schools.

Some enthusiastic Nazi Protestants set up a new Nazi church called the **German Christian Movement**, while Hitler approved the creation of a pagan anti-Christian church called the '**Faith Movement**'. Hitler's ultimate aim was the replacement of Christianity with Nazism.

Top Tip

Have a look back through this unit. At each key point think about whether Hitler could have been stopped. Then consider reasons why was not. This can really help you understand why things actually turned out the way that they did.

Quick Test

1. Why might Germans claim that they did not know what was going on in Germany?

2. Why did no one try to overthrow Hitler until late in the war?

3. In what ways could Germans resist Nazism passively?

4. Why were the churches difficult for the Nazis to deal with? In what ways did some Christians oppose Nazism? What agreement did the Catholic Church sign with the Nazis?

Did you hit your target for this topic? Give yourself a mark out of ten.

Answers 1. Censorship and propaganda prevented them from seeing the truth **2.** Members of the army had taken an oath of loyalty to Hitler. **3.** Attending secret meetings, refusing to salute or to join the Nazi Party. **4.** Many Nazi supporters were church members as were the majority of Germans; some spoke out against them; the Catholic Church and the Nazis signed a 'Concordat' agreeing to tolerate each other.

Enquiry skills

Study the sources below and answer the questions which follow. You should use your own knowledge where appropriate.

CREDIT

Source A is an extract from the memoirs of a Jewish woman, Alice Solomon. It describes the treatment of a Jewish child at school in 1935.

> One day she came home humiliated. 'It was not so nice today', she said. What had happened? The teacher had placed the Aryan children to one side of the classroom and the non-Aryans to the other. The teacher told the Aryans to study the appearance of the others and to point out the marks of their Jewish race. They stood separated as if by a gulf. Children who had played together as friends the day before were now enemies.

1. How useful is Source A as evidence of the treatment of Jewish children in Nazi Germany?

4 marks

Source B is from a German newspaper of 1919.

> The deaths of Rosa Luxemburg and Liebknecht were the proper reward for the blood bath they unleashed. The result of her own actions killed the woman. The day of judgement of Luxemburg and Liebknecht is over. Germany can breathe again. The Spartacists were criminals pure and simple.

2. Discuss the attitude of Source B towards the Spartacists   4 marks

In this 'attitude' question, the rubric (the information given outside the source) is of limited value. Instead, you need to say something about the Spartacist revolt that formed the immediate context in which this newspaper article was written. Link what you have to say to specific points made in the source itself.

Top Tip
In answering 'How useful?' questions, such as this one, it is good to say something about the provenance of the source; Who wrote it? Why was it written? What kind of source is it? When was it written? However, a common mistake is to forget to link points about provenance to the question. How do these things either make it very useful or limited in usefulness in some way? Don't forget to point out the points that the source fails to make.

In **Source C** a modern historian discusses Germany under the Weimar Republic.

> *The first five years of the Weimar Republic were violent ones. Almost every week there were strikes and riots.*
>
> *Many Germans were terrified of communism. Millions of Germans also thought that the Socialists who governed the country were little better than the Communists. They called the Socialists 'November Criminals' and said that they had 'stabbed Germany in the back' by making peace in 1918.*

3. How fully does Source B show reasons for discontent under the Weimar Republic? You should use your own knowledge and give reasons for your answer.   5 marks

Source D is part of a speech by Hitler in July 1933.

> *If anyone criticises me and asks me why I do not use the regular courts of justice, all I say to him is this: I am responsible for the fate of the German people. I am supreme judge for the German people!*

4. How valuable is Source C as evidence about Hitler's ideas on German Law?

3 marks

Top Tip

There are five marks for this question. Aim to take at least two points from the source itself and two or three from recalled knowledge to make your five points. It is better to turn points you use from the source into your own words to make it clear that you have understood the points. Although it is a secondary source, it does not deal with all of the issues at the time.

Top Tip

Any speech that Hitler made was likely to have been for propaganda purposes, so point out that this was for propaganda. Asking 'How valuable?' is just the same as asking 'How useful?' a source is, so apply the same rules when answering this. What is Hitler trying to make people think of him and of the German courts here?

Index